ONE HUNDRED HILL WALKS AROUND BIRMINGHAM

Also in the same series:

ONE HUNDRED
HILL WALKS AROUND
BIRMINGHAM

THE ESSENTIAL GUIDE

RICHARD SHUREY

Series Editor
JOHN CHALMERS

MAINSTREAM
PUBLISHING
EDINBURGH AND LONDON

First published in Great Britain in 1994 by
MAINSTREAM PUBLISHING COMPANY
(EDINBURGH) LTD
7 Albany Street
Edinburgh EH1 3UG
ISBN 1 85158 618 0

A catalogue record for this book is available from the British Library

Typeset in Times by Litho Link Ltd., Welshpool, Powys, Wales
Printed in Great Britain by the Cromwell Press, Melksham, Wiltshire

CONTENTS

Map of Areas

ABOUT THIS BOOK

If thou art worn and hard beset
With sorrows that thou wouldst forget
If thou wouldst read a lesson that will keep
Thy heart from fainting and thy soul from sleep,
Go to the woods and hills; no tears
Dim the sweet look that nature wears.

Spurred by words by Longfellow, this book is presented as a guide to upland country walks – nature's own tranquillisers and antidote to the pressures of everyday life in an often troubled world.

There are, of course, no limits in this age of easy travel to mountains and hills which beckon: a few years ago a trip to the Scottish hills or the Lake District was the very edge of our horizons – today it can be the Appalachians or the foothills of the Himalayas and Nepal.

Our Midland Everests are more modest but none the less enjoyable (and therapeutic) for all that. The hills of Birmingham are in the main gentle slopes – often only a few hundred feet high. But they have one thing in common with the highest in the world: although climbing them takes some effort, there is always a lovely view from the summit. This perhaps is a better reason for climbing Everest than the classical answer – 'because it's there'.

When I started on the daunting task of identifying the 100 hills around Birmingham for this book, I was soon impressed by the immense variety from which to choose. Consider the tail end of the Pennine range or the foothills of the Welsh borderlands and the wood-clothed heights above deep river valleys. There are bare heathlands (for example in Sutton Park or on Cannock Chase) just a few miles from the city centre and Country Park hills.

Perhaps my personal favourites are the lovely Cotswolds. These typify to me all that is best in the countryside of England – the amalgam of hills and woods and quiet ways to villages of mellowed stone which seems to be part of the natural scene.

The walks in this book are not long-distance hikes merely to bag strenuous mile after strenuous mile. (I have heard of folk who punish themselves for 50 hard miles on their 50th birthday – just what to prove, I am uncertain.)

Here are excursions for those who like to amble gently along, taking note of and appreciating the immense beauty of the rural vista (still lovely in spite of all the modern environmental hazards). There are fascinating things to see on the way, ancient buildings to discover, the flora and fauna to identify. There is the idle chatter of shared experiences with a companion, the chance to photograph the scene for reliving the journey later, and perhaps a visit to a friendly inn.

Unfortunately we have no legal right to roam the hills freely in England – the walker is required to keep to the definitive rights of way. Sometimes, therefore, the high summit has to be skirted around but it should not mar the enjoyment of the walks.

So, on with the walking boots – the dog is eager too – and let's set out 'over the hills and far away'.

NOTES

1. The sketch maps are to give a quick visual idea of each walk. They are not to a constant scale and do not replace the relevant Ordnance Survey maps. However, the sketch map and the relevant text should usually enable the walker to cover the route without difficulty, but carrying a copy of the OS map will add to the enjoyment of the walk. In the text of each walk the first map number quoted refers to the Ordnance Survey Landranger Series map (1:50,000 scale). The second number refers to the Ordnance Survey Pathfinder Series (1:25,000 scale).

2. The distance of the walk is approximate – it can vary somewhat when deviations are made to visit inns, churches and interesting features, etc. Distances within the text are also approximate and meant for guidance only.

3. Please remember that the countryside is constantly changing so you may find variations from what is written in the text. While every endeavour has been made to be accurate in all details and to give routes only along definitive rights of way, should any errors have crept in we apologise for these in advance. No responsibility can be accepted for any loss, etc. caused by any inaccuracy.

4. It is difficult to give a time for each walk as walking pace is very varied and often dependent on the weather or the beauty of the view. ('What is this life if full of care, we have no time to stand and stare.') However, a good average is two miles an hour.

ABBREVIATIONS

km	kilometres
ml	miles
ft	feet
NT	National Trust

SYMBOLS ON SKETCH MAPS

Parking place and start of walk

Route of walk

Building

Deciduous woods

Conifer woods

Church with tower

Church with spire

Path or track

Road or lane

Railway

Canal

Stream or river

Castle

THE WALKS

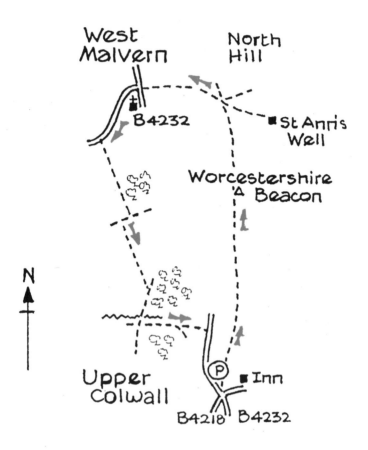

WALK 1

WORCESTERSHIRE

1. *Malvern Hills (North)*

Distance of walk: 9km/5ml.
Distance from Birmingham: 60km/37ml.
Ordnance Survey maps: 150 and 1018.
Refreshments: Inn and tea-room, Upper Colwall.
Paths: Good, hard, well-drained tracks – many are way-marked.
Terrain: Gradual climbing over rocky slopes bordered by heather and gorse.
Points of interest: Toposcope on Beacon which commemorates the 60th year of Victoria's reign in 1897; St Ann's Well (historic source of medicinal water).

The walk climbs to Worcestershire Beacon, at 1,374ft the highest point on the Malvern Hills. The uplands are made of some of the oldest rocks in the land – quartz, pink feldspar and mica.

Park at National Trust carpark off B4218 at Wyche Cutting. 768437. From carpark take clear track signed to Worcestershire Beacon. Pass a 'goldmine' sign (where prospecting could prove disappointing). Keep ahead to walk down the saddle between hills. (St Ann's Well is to the right.) Bear left with the height of North Hill (which can be climbed and is a good viewpoint over the Severn valley) on the right.

Follow the path to the B4232 at West Malvern. Cross over to the road opposite (signed to Mathon) and keep on the road

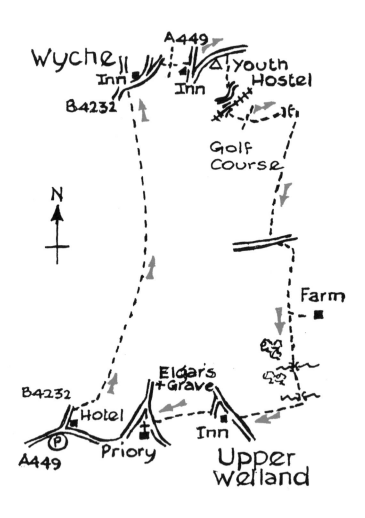

WALK 2

Walk 1   The Worcestershire Beacon

for half a mile. Turn left opposite the drive of Bank Farm. Go down a wide cart-track which leads to a lane. Turn right for 100 yards, then go left down a rough vehicle-way. Past houses climb a stile. Keep ahead to another vehicle-way.

Turn right to a crossing track. Continue left: within 400 yards the vehicle-way twists right. Keep ahead along a path which climbs to a road. Turn right to the starting place.

The route cannot easily be shortened.

2.   Malvern Hills (Central)

Distance of walk: 12km/7.5ml.
Distance from Birmingham: 65km/41ml.
Ordnance Survey maps: 150 and 1018.
Refreshments: Inns, Wyche and Upper Welland; hotel by carpark.
Paths: Well-used tracks on ridge. Paths not clearly defined over farmland.
Terrain: Malverns very hard rock which drains well. Lower parts of walk over clay can be muddy.

15

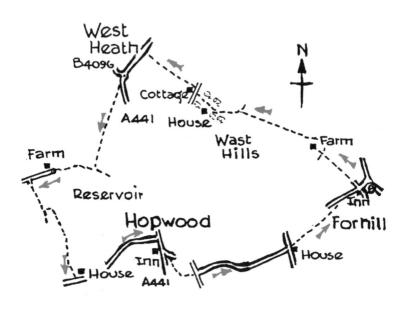

WALK 3

Points of interest: Hills over which Elgar walked; the singer
Jenny Lind lived at house at starting place.

Route follows the lower ridge between the two high peaks of
Worcestershire and Herefordshire Beacons.

Park at British Camp off A449. 763404. Walk a few steps
along the B4232. Take path on right (middle of three ways).
Turn left to walk at back of house to rocky ridge. Route borders
Dyke to road. Turn right then bear right along Old Wyche Road.
After half a mile take unsigned path right. Descend to road.
Take path down steps to road by inn. Steps opposite to road.
Turn left. Past youth hostel turn right down vehicle-track. Keep
ahead at road. By house no. 63 keep ahead along bridleway
under railway to gate to golf course. Follow blue arrows to
junction of tracks. Go left over brook then right through wood.
Over golf course follow arrowed direction to route of disused
railway. Turn right beside embankment. On farm drive turn
right under bridge and immediately left along track to road.
After 400 yards turn right (Shuttlefast Lane). When this goes
left to a farm keep ahead into field. Maintain direction. Cross
bridge. At next turn go right and walk through fields to road.
Turn right then left (Watery Lane). Over brook turn right and at
once left. Keep stream on left. Through gate is large field. Aim
for church. On road turn right then left (A449) to carpark.

To shorten walk: Turn left on road at end of ridge walk.
Pick up track parallel to road. Saves five miles.

3. Wast Hills

Distance of walk: 11km/7ml.
Distance from Birmingham: 9.5km/6ml.
Ordnance Survey maps: 139 and 954.
Refreshments: Inns, Forhill and Hopwood.
Paths: Good, well-trodden tracks; part of route is N Worcs.
Path.
Terrain: Clay heavy going in places; much of area is pasture.
Points of interest: Picnic site Forhill; Upper Bittell Reservoir
(built 1832 to top up waterway) attracts wildfowl; Worcs.
and Birmingham Canal (completed 1815).

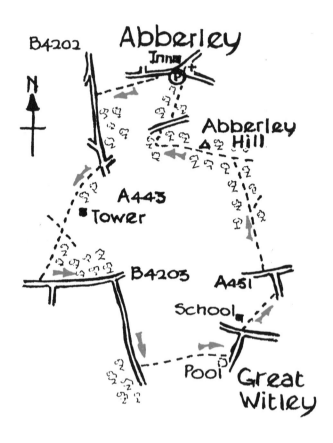

WALK 4

These are 'the forgotten hills of Birmingham'. Although on the S doorstep of city, they are in quiet countryside. At one time the hills posed a problem to canal makers who built a one-and-a-half-mile tunnel underneath them. Park at Forhill picnic area. 055756.

Walk along Lea End Road then go right (signed Forhill House). Climb stile on right. In pasture turn left. Join cart-track then follow path past pool to tarmac vehicle-way along top of Wast Hills. Turn left. Near gates to garden bear right through woods to stile to field and lane. Next path is opposite. Follow track to A441. Turn left past junction, still on A441. Cross road at footpath sign. Follow waymarked path through fields to junction of paths by Upper Bittell Reservoir. Turn right at borders of fields to farm drive to junction. Turn left (Lower Bittell). After 400 yards climb stile left. Go along top of reservoir then through a meadow to lane. Turn left to main road. Go right then along lane on left. Take footpath on right. Go by field to lane junction. Take Stonehouse Lane to T-junction. Opposite is path. Follow signed way over stiles to climb through fields then woods to road. Forhill is right.

To shorten walk: Turn left at junction of paths by reservoir. Follow path to main road. Cross to lane. Saves two miles.

4. *Abberley Hills*

Distance of walk: 9km/6ml.
Distance from Birmingham: 51km/32ml.
Ordnance Survey maps: 150 and 973.
Refreshments: Inn, Abberley.
Paths: Good, well-used tracks; part of route uses Worcestershire Way.
Terrain: On hills route is through woods (lovely in autumn); hills of hard stone drain well.
Points of interest: Old St Michael's Church (part ruined) is Norman building on Saxon site; Manor Arms Inn (which once brewed its own beer) has fine exterior display of arms of local families; lofty Gothic clock tower ('Jones's folly') built in 1883; 'new' St Michael's church dates from 1877.

Walk 2   The ridge from British Camp

Walk 4   Clock tower (Jones's folly) at Abberley

Abberley Hills comprises steep-sided ridge which is mainly woodland but with extensive quarrying of stone on eastern end. There was coal mining up to fourteenth century. Below slopes it is said that St Augustine met the Welsh Bishops in 603 – spot is marked by old oak tree. This walk can be combined with the walk over Woodbury Hill for longer route.

Limited car parking opposite Manor Arms, Abberley. 751676. From centre of Abberley walk along lane with the inn on right side. Near junction take path on left to B4202. Turn left to join A443. Opposite lane turn right along drive of Abberley Hall (mansion now houses school). Keep ahead at junctions to the B4203. Turn left then take the second lane on right. Within half a mile drop down to brook and climb stile on left. The path follows brook downstream to road. Turn left to road junction. Right of opposite health centre, path starts over stile to road. Turn left then left at junction. Take a bridleway (signed Shavers End). Beyond orchards track divides. Leave bridleway to keep ahead along path to hilltop. Turn left at a T-junction of tracks, now walking along Worcestershire Way to pass trig plinth. Descend to lane. Turn right then left along path signed.

The walk cannot be conveniently shortened.

Walk 5   The old oast houses once used to dry hops

WALK 5

5. Suckley Hills

Distance of walk: 11km/7ml.
Distance from Birmingham: 64km/40ml.
Ordnance Survey maps: 150 and 995.
Refreshments: Inns, Alfrick.
Paths: Generally good and well used; part of route is Worcestershire Way.
Terrain: Sandstone hills drain well but the lower tracks can be heavy going. Quiet lanes also used.
Points of interest: Nature reserves at Ravenshills and by Leigh Brook; site of disused railway route; Norman work in Alfrick church which has a shingle tower; former oast houses (now desirable dwellings).

In the *Dictionary of English Place Names* 'Suckley' means 'the uplands covered in woods where birds reside'. This is so apt – not only are these modest hills overlooking Worcestershire so typical of English country scenery, but below slopes at Ravenshills is a nature reserve where birds and wildlife really do reign.

Park at roadside in Alfrick village. 748529. Walk through churchyard of Alfrick church to a kissing gate to field. Walk to corner-stile on far side. On road turn right then left to Woodland Reserve. Walk along lane to Lulsley and keep ahead at two junctions. Two hundred yards further turn left up bridleway (Worcestershire Way). A field is reached and walk along right-hand border to wood. Keep ahead to sheep pastures. In far corner pass through gates then continue with woods on left. The clear path goes through wood to lane at Crews Hill. Turn right then take signed path on left through woods. When path divides take right-hand fork. At blue gate climb stile and continue to clearing. At junction of paths keep ahead to waymark post. Turn right (off main track) to lane. Turn left to T-junction. Turn left and bear right at junction. Almost opposite nature reserve turn left along farm drive. After 400 yards bear right up banked bridleway past farm to Alfrick.

To shorten walk: Turn left at Crews Hill – saves three miles.

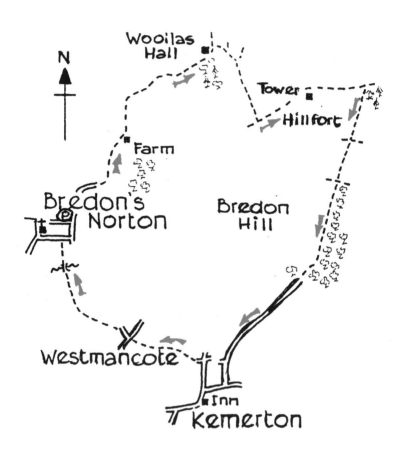

WALK 6

6. Bredon Hill (West)

Distance of walk: 12.3km/6ml.
Distance from Birmingham: 57km/36ml.
Ordnance Survey maps: 150 and 1042.
Refreshments: Inn, Kemerton.
Paths: Most are clear on the ground and well walked.
Terrain: Well-drained soils; the climbs are mainly gradual but steeper sections near summit of hill.
Points of interest: Bredon's Norton's church dates from Norman times; Woollas Hall has associations with the Civil War; Iron Age fort on Bredon Hill; King and Queen stones feature in local folklore; folly tower.

Bredon Hill is an outlier of the Cotswolds and therefore the landscape and terrain have the characteristics of limestone countryside. The buildings are of a lovely butter-hued stone. Traditionally the uplands supported intensive sheep farming.

Park at quiet roadsides in Bredon's Norton. 933390. Go along lane signed no-through road. This becomes cart-track and rises to give views over the Avon vale. Pass buildings and farmsteads to drive of Woollas Hall. Just beyond gateway, climb stile to meadow on right. Continue (walking between two trees) to metal gate to cart-track. After about 300 yards track twists sharp left. Climb step-stile on right. Walk to gate in the far diagonal corner. Keep on same direction along banked way. A metal stile leads to track to summit plateau. Turn left along bridleway track to pass tower and earthworks of fort. Keep along escarpment (left-hand wall). At little fir wood turn right. Keep ahead, crossing other ways to eventually enter wood through bridle gate. Continue to lane to Kemerton. On main road go right then right again. At crossroads turn left to continue along signed footpath to Westmancote. Proceed along Farm Lane. At the end, footpath is signed to Bredon's Norton.

To shorten walk: Turn right along bridleway on top of Bredon. Saves three miles.

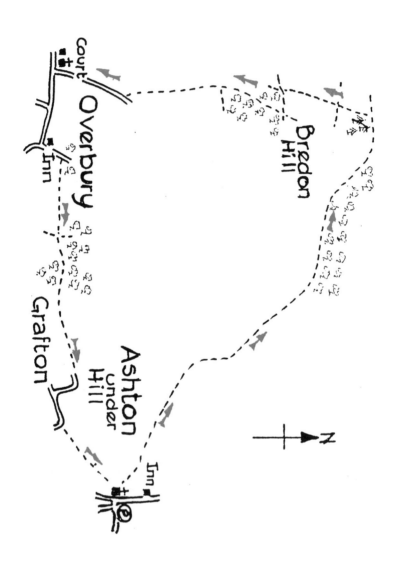

Court

Overbury

Inn

Bredon
Hill

N

Grafton

Ashton
under
Hill

Inn

WALK 7

7. *Bredon Hill (South)*

Distance of walk: 11km/7ml.
Distance from Birmingham: 57km/36ml.
Ordnance Survey maps: 150 and 1042.
Refreshments: Inns, Ashton under Hill and Conderton.
Paths: Usually good on uplands; on lower slopes not always
  clearly defined. Part of route is the Wychavon Way.
Terrain: Bredon Hill is limestone and drains well. The soils
  on lowlands are sometimes of clinging clay.
Points of interest: Herds of deer may be seen; Ashton church
  is Norman; there are 16 other 'listed' buildings in Ashton;
  fourteenth-century stone cross; Overbury Court –
  eighteenth-century mansion.

The southern slopes of Bredon are more gentle than the steep
escarpment of the north. They face the Cotswold ridge so
good views from the 900ft (275m) summit. Bredon Hill has
inspired many writers – the best known are A. E. Housman,
with his 'Summertime on Bredon' and William Cobbett.
When Cobbett passed on one of his 'Rural Rides' he called
the vista 'one of the very richest spots in England'.

Park at quiet roadside in Ashton under Hill. 997377. From
church walk through churchyard and pass through kissing
gate. Follow waymarked route of Wychavon Way indicated
by yellow areas and 'W' signs. Path gradually climbs hill
through fields. After two miles walk alongside right-hand
woods and keep ahead along scarp edge. After small wood
of fir trees on left turn left. Walk by wall (on left) and stay on
constant heading to go over crossing cart-track to junction of
bridleways. Turn left then right after 300 yards. Walk along
wide vehicle-way to descend to join lane to Overbury. Turn
left at T-junction to Conderton. Turn left by inn; take path
signed on right after 200 yards which goes along farm track.
Maintain constant heading, crossing brooks and through
wood and fields to reach Grafton and lane. Follow this to
signed footpath on left. The path leads to Ashton under Hill.

The walk cannot be conveniently shortened.

Elmley Castle

Inn Inn

Tower Castle Site

Bredon Hill

Farm

N

WALK 8

8. Bredon Hill (East)

Distance of walk: 8km/5ml.
Distance from Birmingham: 57km/36ml.
Ordnance Survey maps: 150 and 1042.
Refreshments: Inns, Elmley Castle.
Paths: Good tracks which can be muddy in places. The route
uses 'The Wychavon Way'.
Terrain: Limestone with mixture of pastures, arable land,
woods and scrubland. Climbs are modest gradients.
Points of interest: Elmley Castle is pretty village with inn
which commemorates the visit of Queen Elizabeth I.
Norman church (St Mary's) has work of the twelfth
century. Site of Norman castle (in ruins by early 1400s) on
spur of Bredon Hill. Ancient wayside cross.

The hill rises to almost 1,000ft and was immortalised in A. E.
Housman's poem 'Summertime on Bredon'. It is a weather fore-
caster for surrounding villages, for a local rhyme goes
'When Bredon Hill puts on his hat, Men of the Vale beware of
that'.
    Park at quiet roadside at Elmley Castle. 983414. Go along
lane by Queen Elizabeth Inn which is signed as no-through
road. Follow hill lane to end. Keep ahead along banked track.
Continue to hill pasture and walk by the left-hand borders
then follow winding way through bushes. There are herds of
deer in this area. Follow path to top of hill and turn right
along escarpment past little fir wood (on left) to tower (built
by Mr Parsons of Kemerton to take height of hill over
1,000ft). Retrace steps to fir wood. Turn right (wood now on
left). Cross farm track and continue to junction of tracks.
Turn left and cross tarmac farm road. Keep ahead, leaving
main way to go alongside plantation of Scots pines. Pick up
line of fir trees then turn left to broad track by wood. Cross
this track to pick up waymark signs on Wychavon Way. Path
descends through woodlands then over wide banked way.
Bear right to go through scrubland. Keep following waymark
signs. A stream is crossed then path hugs border of field to
lane. Turn left to Elmley Castle.

Great
Comberton

Farm

N

Tower
Fort

Banbury
Stone

Bredon Hill

WALK 9

To shorten walk: Turn left on reaching the top of escarpment. Saves two miles.

9. Bredon Hill (North)

Distance of walk: 6.5km/4ml.
Distance from Birmingham: 57km/36ml.
Ordnance Survey maps: 150 and 1042.
Refreshments: Should be carried.
Paths: Good, clear tracks marked at roads.
Terrain: Bredon Hill is limestone outlier of Cotswolds. Route through woods and farmland (arable and pasture).
Points of interest: Eighteenth-century folly tower on summit (built by Mr Parsons of Kemerton); Celtic hill-fort; folklore stones (Banbury and 'King and Queen'); castle site; Great Comberton's church is Norman.

The walk climbs the northern scarp edge of Bredon Hill with increasingly magnificent views over the Vale of Evesham and snake-like River Avon.

Park in quiet roadsides in village of Great Comberton. 957422. Near church take path signed Elmley Castle. Climb stile and follow track at edge of fields. Go over step-stile and brook, then further stiles and another brook. The direction is fairly constant then go over third bridge to right to cross ditch to arable field. Look for new stile in distant top corner to farm cart-track. Turn right. Stay on farm track to climb through woods and pastures to top of hill. By wood pick up bold track and turn right alongside left-hand wire fence with steep scarp edge of hill now on right. Pass through gate by little fir wood. Keep ahead to visit folklore rocks, folly tower and hill-fort. Retrace steps. Look for stone stile left. Descend hill alongside wire fence. Climb corner-stile to sheep pasture and keep downhill to second corner-stile. Go along cart-track to farm. Follow right of way which goes alongside the drive (keep on left) to Great Comberton.

This walk cannot be shortened.

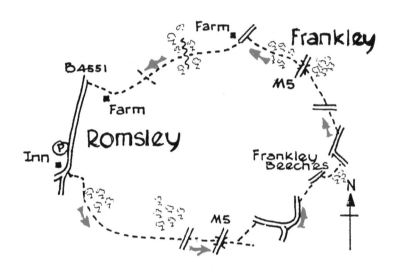

WALK 10

10. *Frankley Beeches*

Distance of walk: 11km/7ml.
Distance from Birmingham: 13km/8ml.
Ordnance Survey maps: 933 and 953.
Refreshments: Inns, Romsley.
Paths: Sometimes difficult and not well used.
Terrain: Pasture and arable fields in undulating countryside.
Points of interest: Frankley Beeches; old rail route.

The clump of wind-smoothed beeches on top of a knoll is a distinctive feature of the countryside on the western borders of Birmingham. The hill was a gift from the Cadbury family.

Park at roadsides in Romsley. 963796. From Romsley school walk along B4551. Turn left down signed path by house no. 80. In pasture walk to stile opposite. Continue by ditch to wood. Bear right (trees on left) to step-stile to next field. Maintain direction to join cart-track. Pass through gateway. Bear left over open field to stile then continue to another. Walk alongside hedge to double stile to next field. Stay by left border through gateway. Bear left. Walk by pond and go through metal gate. Climb hill. Continue to lane. Cross to vehicle-way. Go under motorway. Keep ahead then turn left over wide bridge and stile to field. Walk through field over tractor-way to bridge and stile. Keep heading to lane. Turn right then take two lefts at junctions. Four hundred yards further climb fence stile to field. Cut off corner to road. Turn road then climb hill of Frankley Beeches.

Continue to lane. Turn left, passing junction. Go through gateway left. Cut corner off field. On lane cross to gate to field. Walk by right-hand border then at border of wood. Rather hidden track through trees to far side of wood. Turn right to concrete drive under motorway. Climb stile by gate and walk directly away from the motorway. Walk at sides of fields. Enter woods through gate. Track is straight through trees to cart-track. Turn right. Pass in front of white house and through gate. Turn left. Keep farm on right to step-stile. Turn right and cross brook. Turn slightly right. Continue down rough pasture and keep heading through gateway.

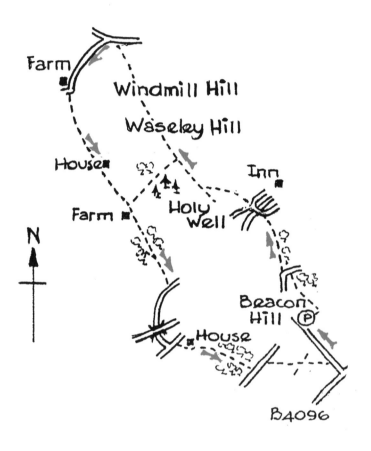

Farm

Windmill Hill

Waseley Hill

House

Inn

Farm

Holy
Well

N

Beacon
Hill

House

B4096

WALK 11

Cross brook and climb stile. Follow waymarked direction. Veer slight left to fence on top of hill. Keep ahead to corner stile. Follow direction to keep farm left to B4551. Romsley is left.

The walk cannot easily be shortened.

11. Lickey Hills (South)

Distance of walk: 9km/6ml.
Distance from Birmingham: 14km/9ml.
Ordnance Survey maps: 139 and 953.
Refreshments: Inn, Rubery; tea-room Windmill Hill.
Paths: Good – clear and well used.
Terrain: Pastureland on hills; lower tracks can be muddy.
Points of interest: Beacon 'castle' with toposcope; toposcope on Windmill Hill; visitor centre below Windmill Hill; Chadwick Manor (nineteenth-century mansion).

Walk starts at Beacon Hill (at 987ft the highest point of the Lickeys). It was a firing station in an old early-warning communications system and was used to warn of the Spanish Armada. The hill has been used in more modern times for celebrations such as the present Queen's coronation.

Park at Beacon Hill carpark off B4096. From carpark walk to beacon 'castle' and turn left along the escarpment to lane. Turn left. On bend turn right along bridleway. At road turn left over A38 to Holywell. Go left then right through carpark. Bear left up hill then follow ridge path to right. By gates is junction of paths. Keep ahead over Waseley and Windmill Hills to carpark and visitor centre of Country Park. On road go left then left at junction. Follow lane past farm and keep ahead along path. Past house continue to junction of paths by farm. Climb stile to field. Walk to far end. Climb stile to woods and maintain the heading through the trees and along farm 'road' to lane. Turn right under main road to T-junction. Turn left then at once right along house drive. Continue by house and ahead to woods. Climb the hill to lane. Turn left then right over stile. The clear path over fields leads to road. Turn left to carpark.

To shorten walk: At junction of paths by gates turn left. Saves two miles.

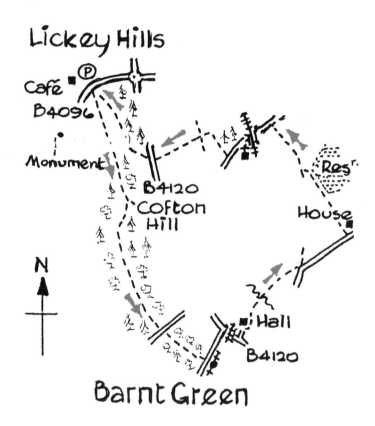

WALK 12

12. Lickey Hills (North)

Distance of walk: 9km/6ml.
Distance from Birmingham: 13km/8ml.
Ordnance Survey maps: 139 and 953/954.
Refreshments: Inn, Barnt Green; café by carpark.
Paths: Good – well marked and well used.
Terrain: The hills are of hard rock which drains well; lowland
   tracks can be muddy at times.
Points of interest: Monument (90ft high) to Lord Plymouth:
   old dew ponds; Bittell Reservoir (built to top up canal in
   late eighteenth century) attracts wildfowl; Rose and
   Crown old coaching inn by carpark; Cofton Church with
   bellcot 600 years old.

These uplands have been called the 'Hills of Birmingham',
although in fact they lie outside the city boundaries. Under
the enclosures of last century, there was a danger that
ordinary folk would be excluded. However, a few public-
spirited persons decided to purchase urgently what land they
could; further acres were donated by the Cadbury family and
others. By early 1920s there was a natural reserve of
450 acres.

Use carpark at Lickey Hills Country Park off B4096.
995758. From carpark cross B4096 to signed footpath over
brook (infant River Arrow). Do not climb log steps but keep
ahead along wide track. Maintain heading beyond visitor
centre and grassed area to again walk along wide track
through trees. At fork stay on main track which bears right
then resumes old direction to lane. Cross directly over along
path to road by station at Barnt Green. Turn left to B4120.
Turn right under railway then at once left along estate road.
At far end take path behind sports hall. In pasture walk by
left-hand hedge then go over brook and into next field. Bear
right over open field to road. Turn left for 400 yards. Take
signed path on left. Walk at edge of field and keep ahead to
stile to Bittell Reservoir. Go along dam then bear left to stile
to vehicle-way. Turn right then left at road. Just past Cofton
Church take path on right. Follow clear path to cross another

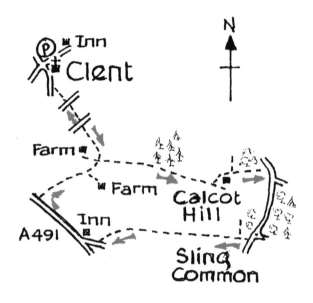

WALK 13

path. Keep ahead to B4120. Cross to opposite path. Climb to ridgetop. Bear right to path to steps down to outward track.

To shorten walk: At B4120 early on route turn left. Saves two-and-a-half miles.

13. Calcot Hill

Distance of walk: 8km/5ml.
Distance from Birmingham: 19km/12ml.
Ordnance Survey maps: 139 and 953.
Refreshments: Inns and restaurant, Clent.
Paths: Good, signed paths, some waymarked. Part of route on North Worcs. long-distance path.
Terrain: Mainly sandy, well-drained soils; many paths are over pastures and heathlands – others use cart-tracks.
Points of interest: Clent church has fine barrel-roof and tower is fifteenth century; Vine Inn was once water mill; part of walk over National Trust land.

This is a gentle hill but with splendid views over Worcestershire towards Malvern ridge. We walk alongside one of many brooks which once powered the numerous scythe and sword mills of Belbroughton. The hill is named after Richard de Calcote, an eighteenth-century lord of the manor.

Park at quiet roadsides in Clent. 929794. From church walk along lane signed Walton Pool. Within quarter of a mile there is path on left. Cut off corner of pasture to lane. Cross to drive opposite. Walk along drive for 100 yards then continue along path to lane. Again cross to opposite path. In field keep ahead then bear right to stile to cart-track. Turn left and follow track which climbs to former farmhouse on top of Calcot Hill. Leave the vehicle-way to climb stile on left. Way is signed to meeting of paths by another stile to reach waymarked North Worcs. Path. Keep ahead alongside left-hand wire fence then go by waymark post. The path borders wood. Climb stiles to lane. Turn right to walk alongside brook and keep ahead at junctions. Take vehicle-track on right signed as footpath to Hollies Hill. Follow track to lane;

WALK 14

turn right to A491. Turn right for half a mile. Just past layby path starts (signed Walton Pool). Path is straight to farm drive. Keep ahead to cart-track and retrace steps of outward route to Clent.

The walk cannot conveniently be shortened.

14. Woodbury Hill

Distance of walk: 6km/4ml.
Distance from Birmingham: 51km/32ml.
Ordnance Survey maps: 150 and 973.
Refreshments: Hotel, Green Witley.
Paths: Well-used paths over fields and through woods; part of route is along Worcestershire Way.
Terrain: Well-drained soils; route is over pasture and scrubland. On Woodbury Hill paths are through mixed woodland.
Points of interest: Iron Age camp mounds and hollows; Hundred House Hotel was Georgian posting house; Chapel given to Great Witley in 1882.

The wooded knoll is an outlier of Abberley Hill and tops 900ft. The summit is crowned by the earthworks of an Iron Age fort. In 1405 the Welsh leader Owen Glendower glowered across to Abberley for several days where Henry IV had set up camp. A most interesting place to visit after the walk is Witley Court, a huge ruined mansion with splendid weatherworn fountains. The nearby church (which escaped the destructive fire) is the finest example of Baroque work in England.

Use carpark at junction of A443 and B4197 in Great Witley. 757657. From carpark cross to B4197. Within 300 yards take path on right. Walk past pools and keep at edges of field to step-stile to lane. Turn right to B4203 then left. After half a mile take lane on left. Within a few steps climb stile to sheep pastures on left. (Now on Worcestershire Way.) Follow arrowed direction to climb the side of Walsgrove Hill. Beyond climb stile to scrubland then woods. When path divides go right to lane. Turn left. Just past house take signed

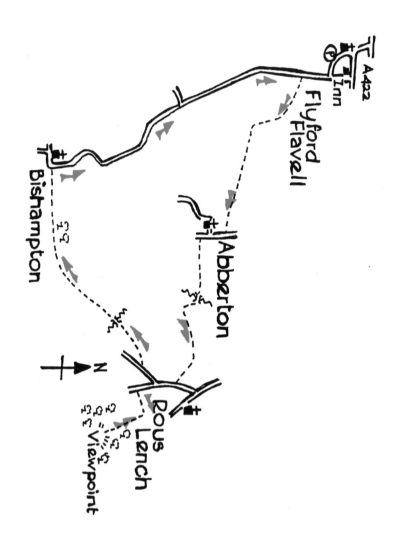

WALK 15

path on left. The track is through woods to meadow. Leave Worcestershire Way (which goes over stile right). Climb rough stile by gate. The path now runs just inside woods as it skirts Woodbury Hill. Through black gate (few hundred yards before buildings) turn left. At T-junction of tracks go right then left at next junction. Walk along forest 'road' and keep ahead along path to descend to lane. Cross to outward path to return to Great Witley.

The walk cannot conveniently be shortened.

15.   The Lenches

Distance of walk: 11km/7ml.
Distance from Birmingham: 42km/26ml.
Ordnance Survey maps: 150 and 996/997.
Refreshments: Inn, Flyford Flavell.
Paths: Some lowland paths not well used and not marked on ground. Part of route uses Wychavon Way.
Terrain: Lowland paths are through arable land – clay soils. There is some lane walking.
Points of interest: Rous Lench Court is magnificent country house occupied by Rous family 1382 to 1721; St Peter's church, Rous Lench, is Norman; moated site of manor behind church; Abberton church spire taken down in 1957 (in flight path of Pershore airfield).

The Lenches are a group of five lovely little villages nestling under gentle hills which have themselves taken on the title and some scholars say that 'Lench' comes from an Old English word for 'ridge' or 'hill'. Many of the slopes are clothed in orchards for the Evesham markets. The route climbs to about 320ft.

Park at quiet roadsides in Flyford Flavell. 979550. From church walk along road to junction by 'Boot Inn'. Turn right (lane signed to Bishampton). After 400 yards turn left down farm track. In field cross to gateway then follow right-hand borders of two further fields. Turn left across pasture to stile and bridge. Wychavon Way signs to lane at Abberton. Turn right. When lane twists sharp right keep ahead along farm

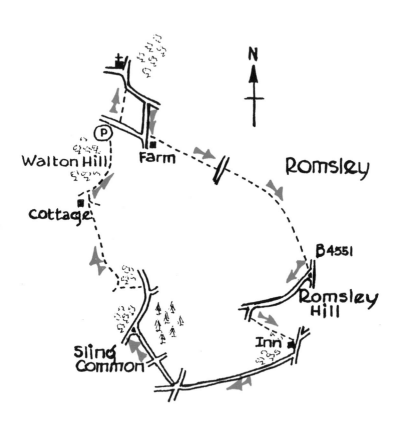

WALK 16

road. Within 300 yards turn left along signed bridleway (blue arrow). Keep ahead to cross bridge over brook. Bear right then left past pool along track to road at Rous Lench. Turn right then left at path after half a mile. The path is signed Wychavon Way. Follow waymarks to enter Yield Wood. The path climbs sharply to viewpoint. Retrace steps to road. Turn right then left at junction. Just past barn go through gate on right. Turn half-left to stile in opposite border. Keep ahead to bridge over stream. Follow water downstream. Nearing church aim towards white cottage. On lane turn right to Flyford Flavell.

The walk cannot conveniently be shortened.

16. Romsley Hill

Distance of walk: 10km/6.5ml.
Distance from Birmingham: 16km/10ml.
Ordnance Survey maps: 139 and 953.
Refreshments: Inns, Romsley.
Paths: Signposts at roads; some tracks not defined on ground.
Terrain: Some soils clay and going heavy in damp conditions.
Points of interest: St Kenelm's Church, historic site where boy king Kenelm was murdered in 819 and waters flowed from holy well; church has much Norman work; attractive pools Sling Common (National Trust).

Romsley Hill sits astride a main road that rises to over 850ft. The wind always seems to blow fresh here – which perhaps was why a large hospital was built on the height. The village church of Romsley was built on the sacred spot of a holy well to which great numbers of pilgrims came for healing.

Park at Walton carpark in Clent Hills Country Park. 943802. Turn right out of carpark. Within few steps along lane climb new stile on left. Track across field is clear to lane. Turn left to church. Retrace steps along lane. Turn right at junction. Just before next junction take signed footpath on left. Walk by right-hand borders of fields to lane. Cross to footpath.

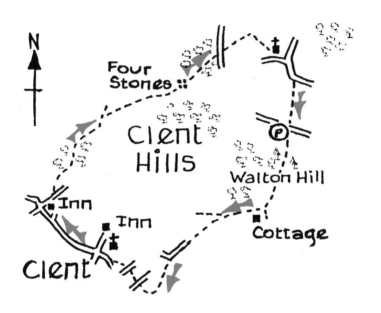

N

Four Stones ::

Clent Hills

Walton Hill

P

Inn

Inn

Cottage

Clent

WALK 17

Follow unmarked path near left-hand edge of pasture to far corner-stile into wood. Out of trees keep on same heading, ignoring crossing paths to road on Romsley Hill. Turn right and bear left (keeping on main road) at junction. Take signed path on left. Follow track to emerge on B4551 by inn. Turn right then at once right along lane. At junction take second road on right and go over at crossroads. Turn right (Sling Common is to left) and at once right again. Just past next junction take path on left over stile. Climb the hill (now on North Worcs. Path). Follow waymarks to carpark over Walton Hill.

To shorten walk: Bear right (along lane) rather than left (along main road) after Romsley Hill – saves one-and-a-half miles.

17.   Clent Hills

Distance of walk: 9km/6ml.
Distance from Birmingham: 16km/10ml.
Ordnance Survey maps: 139 and 953.
Refreshments: Inns and restaurant, Clent.
Paths: Good tracks, many waymarked.
Terrain: Clent Hills are sandstone which drains well. Paths are through woodlands and over heathlands.
Points of interest: The Four Stones on summit look druidical but were set in place by Lord Lyttleton 200 years ago; toposcope to identify landmarks; view of stately home – Hagley Hall; folly castle ruin; St Kenelm's Church named after boy king of Mercia (murdered in 819).

Adams and Walton hills both nudge the 1,000ft contour and form one of the great watersheds of Central England. The name may have come from the Danish 'Klent' – a craggy hill. Much of the land is in National Trust care.

Park at Walton carpark in Clent Hills Country Park. 943802. To left of information board take fenced path marked North Worcs. Path. Path twists up hill to ridge path. Turn left to trig plinth. Bear left to pass waymark post. At junction of ways by cottage take path to right alongside

*Walk 17   The lovely row of beeches along the summit of the
Clent Hills*

fence. Path becomes vehicle-track. A hundred yards beyond
cottage climb stile to field. Keep old direction to corner-stile.
Keep ahead then bear right to go over brow of rise to stile to
lane. Cross to stile and follow path over lane to Clent. At
crossroads by church take lane to Lower Clent. Where lane
divides take left-hand way. By inn turn right. Within 100
yards take bridleway on left. At junction of tracks bear left.
At pool go left and continue past stile (do not climb). Within
step or two take waymarked path on right (North Worcs.
Path). Follow route past viewing platform (presented by AA
in 1985) and continue to summit and Four Stones. Soon leave
arrowed route to keep along ridge. Drop down to lane. Cross
to path and follow series of stiles to St Kenelm's Church. On
lane turn left then right at junction. Within a few hundred
yards there is path on right. Go over field to lane. Carpark is
to right.

To shorten walk: By Clent Church turn right along lane
which climbs to T-junction. Carpark is to right. Saves three
miles.

Walk 22   The River Teme runs in the valley below Rodge Hill

Walk 28   The old water mill

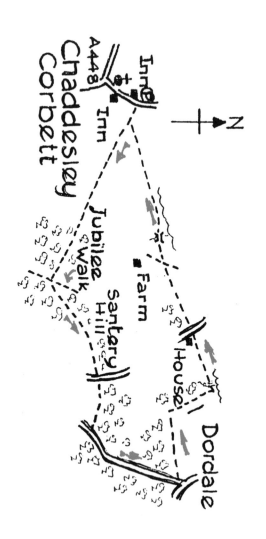

WALK 18

18. Santery Hill, Chaddesley

Distance of walk: 9km/6ml.
Distance from Birmingham: 24km/15ml.
Ordnance Survey maps: 139 and 953.
Refreshments: Inns, Chaddesley Corbett.
Paths: Good and well used. Marked Jubilee Walk through
   woods was designated in 1977 to mark anniversary of
   Queen's reign.
Terrain: Sandy, gravelly soils in woods. Part of route through
   fields and orchards.
Points of interest: Typical Worcestershire black and white
   buildings in Chaddesley; Norman church; nature reserve.

Santery Hill is covered with trees which are part of the
Chaddesley Woods Nature Reserve. This is primarily
managed to perpetuate the traditional oak woodlands.

Park at roadside in Chaddesley Corbett. 893737. Walk
down signed footpath opposite Swan Inn. Keep ahead along
cart-track. When main track turns left maintain old direction
over fields to stile to woods. Keep ahead to climb to junction
of tracks. Turn left then at once right (yellow waymark –
white is Jubilee Walk). In pasture walk at edge of woods to
lane at Santery Hill. Cross to opposite path and continue to
lane. Turn left for half a mile to stile on left. In pasture walk
to far stile and ahead to woods. Turn right. Before corner take
rather hidden path on left. At path junction turn left over
bridge. Turn right over stile. Walk through pastures to road.
Take opposite path (signed Briar Hill). Proceed through
rough pasture to distant fence-stile. After 100 yards veer left
to concealed stile. Turn right. Maintain heading along
unmarked path through hedge gap. Bear right to stile under
pylon. Cross farm drive (no stile). Cross field and brook.
Series of stiles shows way to join outward route.

To shorten walk: Turn left at first lane – saves two miles.

WALK 19

19.   *Stagborough Hill*

Distance of walk: 9km/5ml.
Distance from Birmingham: 38km/24ml.
Ordnance Survey maps: 138 and 952.
Refreshments: Inn, Ribbesford.
Paths: Good tracks; part of route is through Forestry
  Commission woods then alongside River Severn.
Terrain: Well-drained rocks/sand on upland tracks; lower
  slopes can be muddy at times.
Points of interest: Norman church at Areley Kings; Severn is
  busy pleasure waterway.

This modest upland is viewed from a distance on the walk. It
is clothed in woodlands and arable lands in some lovely
countryside overlooking the valley of the River Severn.
   Limited parking by Areley Kings church. 802710. Take
signed path to left of church. Walk alongside the churchyard
(on right side) to path to narrow lane. Turn left to B4194.
Turn right for quarter of a mile. Take signed path on left.
Walk at side of field to fence-stile. Keep ahead through
wood. Climb stile and regain old heading along wide track.
Summit of Stagborough Hill away to right. Stay on same
direction through fields to gate to extensive woodlands. Keep
direction at junctions of forest 'roads' and tracks.
Immediately before stile and gate to lane take path
descending hill to right. Path meets forest 'road'. Keep
walking downhill. Leave forest 'road' by right-hand caravan
site in trees. Take path ahead to B4194 by inn. Turn left on
road for 200 yards. Turn right to take riverside path to A451.
Turn right to lane signed to Areley Kings. Within 400 yards
take lane on left to start.
   The walk cannot conveniently be shortened.

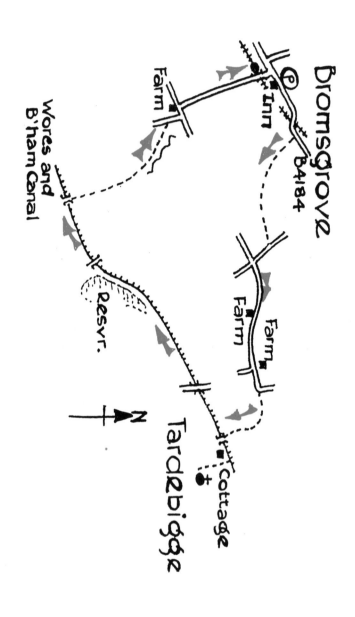

WALK 20

20.   Tardebigge

Distance of walk: 7km/4.5ml.
Distance from Birmingham: 25.5km/16ml.
Ordnance Survey maps: 139 and 974.
Refreshments: Inn, Bromsgrove.
Paths: Good tracks and canal towpath used.
Terrain: Route is through mixed arable and pastoral farmland.
Points of interest: Worcs. and Birmingham Canal (completed in 1812) with famous Tardebigge flight of locks (including deepest narrow lock in country). Eighteenth-century Tardebigge Church.

The hill to Tardebigge caused problems to the canal builders, hence the flight of locks to haul craft up 220ft in two-and-a-half miles. Above the canal is the lovely church (built 1777) with the 135ft-high spire.

Park in roads near Bromsgrove station. 969694. Walk third of a mile along B4184. Just over railway bridge take signed path right. Walk at side of sports field and through sheep pasture with stiles showing the way to lane. Turn right then left at crossroads. Pass old farmhouse and keep ahead at junction. After half a mile, as lane twists 90 degrees left, keep ahead along signed path across arable field. Walk by mounds to cross ditch by bridge.

In meadow climb a stile and follow rivulet downstream a few steps. Bear right to climb bank and climb stile to pasture. Climb field. Go over canal bridge to towpath. Near lock-keeper's cottage climb stile to meadow. Climb ridge aiming to right of church. Retrace steps to canal. Turn left along towpath which passes many locks. After just over a mile leave canal at bridge. Walk away from waterway alongside field boundaries (keep on left then right) to lane. Turn right to T-junction. Go left then at once right. St Godwald's Lane goes to Bromsgrove station.

The walk cannot be shortened.

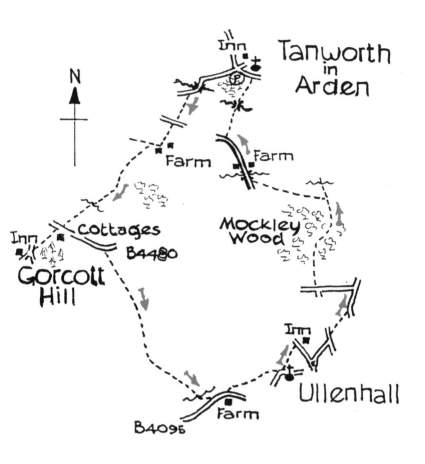

WALK 21

21. Gorcott Hill and Mockley Wood

Distance of walk: 13km/8ml.
Distance from Birmingham: 21km/13ml.
Ordnance Survey maps: 139 and 954/975.
Refreshments: Inns, Gorcott Hill, Tanworth and Ullenhall.
Paths: Some not marked on ground; a little difficult at
  Mockley Wood (paths signed but not always correctly).
Terrain: Route is through mixed farmland and woods. Clay
  soils in places can result in muddy paths at times.
Points of interest: Tanworth is pretty village with Norman
  church and interesting old houses and inn around village
  green.

Gorcott Hill is on a wooded ridge overlooking
Worcestershire; Mockley Wood is attractive at all times but
especially in springtime with carpets of bluebells.

The walk starts at Tanworth in Arden. Park in the street
around the green. 113705. Go along main street. Turn left
along Bates Lane. Within third of a mile climb stile on left.
Walk at edge of field to lane. Turn right a few steps then go
over stile left. Keep at side of field and by barns to farm. Turn
right through gate and along cart-track. Go through second
gate and cut over field on left to far diagonal corner. Maintain
direction in next field, keeping to left of pool. Drop down to
pole-stile and continue to metal gate. Turn right through gate.
Walk length of two fields, going through wire fence. In far
corner go over stile and brook to pasture. Aim towards white
cottages. Go over stile to B4480. Cross to opposite path and
continue to Gorcott Hill.

Retrace steps to B4480. Turn right for 400 yards. Path is
signed by house drive right. Follow left-hand edge of fields,
climbing ahead to climb tall step-stile. Bear left through
corner metal gate behind brick animal shelters. A few steps
further cross brook. Follow edge of meadow to road. Turn
left. Opposite farm climb stile. Follow waymarked path to
Ullenhall. Opposite church take bold path to village. Turn
right then left along lane. Go left at next junction along
Watery Lane. At T-junction go left a few steps. Pass through

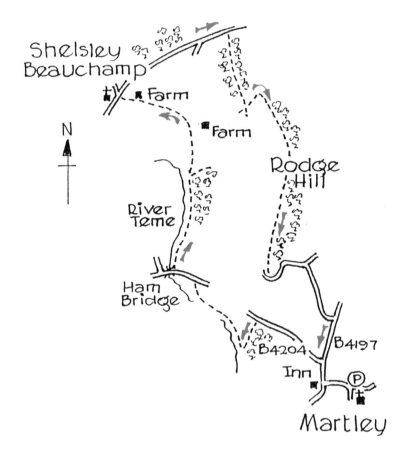

Shelsley
Beauchamp

Farm

N

Farm

Rodge
Hill

River
Teme

Ham
Bridge

B4204

B4197

Inn

Martley

WALK 22

kissing gate. Keep by right edge of field to lane. Turn left then left at junction. Take path right at next road junction. Cross field to pass through gate. Continue through hunting gate. Follow arrowed way through Mockley Wood. Climb stile to meadow. Turn left to far end. Continue over stiles to lane. Turn right. After half a mile take path on right to Tanworth.

The walk cannot easily be shortened.

22. *Rodge Hill*

Distance of walk: 11km/7ml.
Distance from Birmingham: 51km/32ml.
Ordnance Survey maps: 150 and 973.
Refreshments: Inn, Martley.
Paths: Mainly good and well walked; part of route along Worcestershire Way.
Terrain: Mixture of woods, arable and meadowland.
Points of interest: Twelfth-century church at Martley with wall paintings; route to hill is along valley of River Teme.

Park opposite road to church in Martley village. 756599. Drop down B4204 to centre of village by post office. Turn right then left at fork to stay on B4204. A little over half a mile climb stile on left (path signed to Kingswood). Drop down to river and turn right. Follow path to road. Turn left to bridge. Do not cross river but climb stile on right. Again walk beside river. Path goes through woods. Out of the trees gradually leave river. Cross brook to arable field. Walk alongside hedges (on right then left through gates) to join wide cart-track. Go by barns to road by church at Shelsley Beauchamp. Turn right. Just past junction take signed path on right. Follow route of Worcestershire Way along Rodge Hill. On lane turn left then right when road forks to B4197. Martley is to right.

To shorten walk: Take path to right near end of riverside woods – saves two-and-a-half miles.

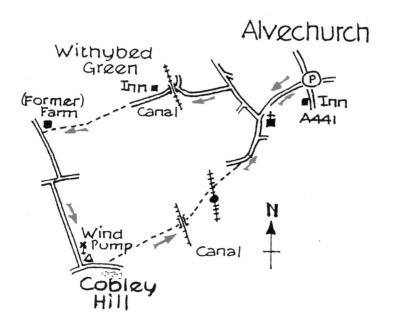

WALK 23

23. Cobley Hill

Distance of walk: 5.5km/3.5ml.
Distance from Birmingham: 14.5km/9ml.
Ordnance Survey maps: 139 and 954.
Refreshment: Inns, Alvechurch.
Paths: Sometimes not defined on ground but route is clear.
Terrain: Walk is mainly over pasture and along lanes.
Points of interest: Norman church at Alvechurch; old black
   and white timbered houses; Birmingham and Worcester
   Canal (completed 1815).

The little hill catches the west wind and can be a breezy spot
– hence the wind pump built on the summit. The engineers
building the Birmingham and Worcestershire canal tunnelled
their waterway for a third of a mile under the lower slopes.

Park in square at Alvechurch or quiet roads off main road.
028726. From square walk along Bear Hill to church.
Opposite go right down Swan Lane then left under railway
and over canal to Withybed Green. Walk past inn and
continue ahead to end of lane. Climb stile to pasture. Keep
ahead over second stile. Climb hill to pass through gate.
Follow way to former farmstead (now converted to houses).
On lane turn left. At junction go right then at once left to
climb Cobley Hill (old wind pump). Turn left at crossroads.
Within 300 yards path is signed on left. In field turn right, so
regaining old heading. Go through gate. Still on same
heading, continue to tunnel under canal. Walk around arable
field to crossing place of railway (station on right). Cross
station road to footpath to road. Turn right to Alvechurch.

The route cannot be shortened.

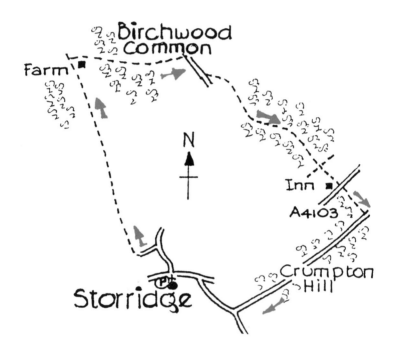

WALK 24

24. Birchwood Common

Distance of walk: 5.5km/3.5ml.
Distance from Birmingham: 59km/37ml.
Ordnance Survey maps: 150 and 995/1018.
Refreshments: Inn on A4103; fruit at fruit farm (summer).
Paths: Good tracks; part of route along Worcestershire Way.
Terrain: Well-drained soils; route is through fruit farms, woods and pastures.
Points of interest: Fruit farms; Elgar wrote *Dream of Gerontius* and *Enigma Variations* at Birchwood Lodge.

The walk is over an area of gentle hills loved by Elgar and always within sight of the loftier Malverns. Many of the slopes are clothed in fruit orchards.

Limited parking by Storridge Church. 748487. Opposite church take lane signed Birchwood. After quarter of a mile turn left along farm road (signed as no-through road). After one-and-a-quarter miles is fruit farm. Immediately after farmhouse turn right (signed Worcestershire Way). Go along cart-track and climb to woods. Continue to follow Worcestershire Way waymarks to eventually walk along vehicle-drive to climb to lane at Birchwood Common. Turn right for quarter of a mile. Climb a stile left. (Birchwood Lodge nearby.) Walk by right-hand wire fence to corner-stile. Follow arrowed way marked 'alternative route'. Continue along waymarked path through pasture and woods. Eventually cross cart-track. Continue at side of arable field to A4103 by inn. Cross to opposite path to lane. Turn right. Lane goes over Crompton Hill (was Cromwell Hill – he mustered troops here before Battle of Worcester) to road. Turn right to A4103.

The walk cannot easily be shortened.

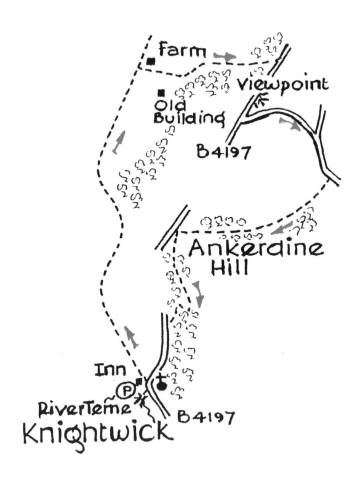

Farm

Viewpoint

Old Building

B4197

Ankerdine Hill

Inn

River Teme

Knightwick

P

B4197

WALK 25

25. *Ankerdine Hill*

Distance of walk: 6.5km/4ml.
Distance from Birmingham: 56km/35ml.
Ordnance Survey maps: 150 and 995.
Refreshments: Inn, Knightwick.
Paths: Mostly well-used tracks but not defined on final climb
   up Ankerdine Hill. Part of route is Worcestershire Way.
Terrain: Mixed woodland, rough pasture and orchard.
Points of interest: Fine views over valleys of rivers Teme and
   Severn. Stone on Knightwick church marks high floods of
   1886.

The walk is up one of the several wooded hills N of the
Malvern ridge.
   Park in cul-de-sac road near the Talbot Inn. 733560. Walk
along the wide cart-track at the right-hand side of the inn.
Keep ahead; the track nudges River Teme. After one-and-a-
half miles and immediately before farmhouse on right turn
right. The grass track gradually climbs and goes through
gates and passes by large fruit trees to right. Into hill pasture

Walk 25   The old cider mill at Knightwick

65

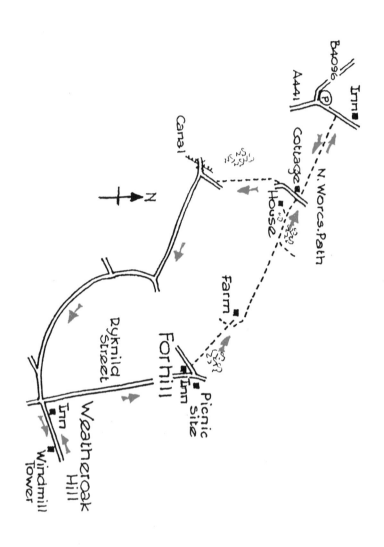

WALK 26

keep ahead (woodlands on right) to woods. Follow well-worn track to B4197. Turn right to top of Ankerdine Hill. Take lane on left. Follow lanes for three-quarters of a mile, going right at junction. Take signed (Worcestershire Way) path through gate right. In pasture walk by left-hand hedge to wood. Turn right (still in field) to gate to wood. Follow waymarks to meadow. Climb to vehicle-track. Turn left. Follow Worcestershire Way signs on twisting path descending steeply to B4197. Turn left to Knightwick.

To shorten walk: Keep on B4197 to pick up later vehicle-track (saves one mile).

26. *Weatheroak Hill*

Distance of walk: 9km/6ml.
Distance from Birmingham: 11km/7ml.
Ordnance Survey maps: 139 and 934.
Refreshments: Inns, Weatheroak, Forhill and by start.
Paths: Good tracks but some not identifiable on the ground.
    Part of route is along North Worcs. Path.
Terrain: Some of the tracks can be muddy as the soils are
    clay.
Points of interest: Picnic site (end of North Worcs. Path);
    Windmill Tower at Weatheroak; end of one-and-a-half-mile-long canal tunnel; Roman road.

This is a steep little upland which gives fine views over the Worcestershire countryside. A pub on the slopes was once a coaching inn where horses were changed.

Park on service road at junction of B4096 and A441. 029768. Turn left along A441 towards Birmingham. Within 100 yards take path over stile on right (signed North Worcs. Path). Walk at edge of field then sports field. Descend to lane by cottage. Turn right. By bend in lane take path on right. Path is almost parallel to lane then rejoins lane near where canal tunnel emerges. At junction turn left. Follow lanes for two miles as map to bottom of Weatheroak Hill. Here Ryknild Street (Roman road – Wall to Stow) crosses. Climb hill past inn left for views. Descend to Roman road. Turn

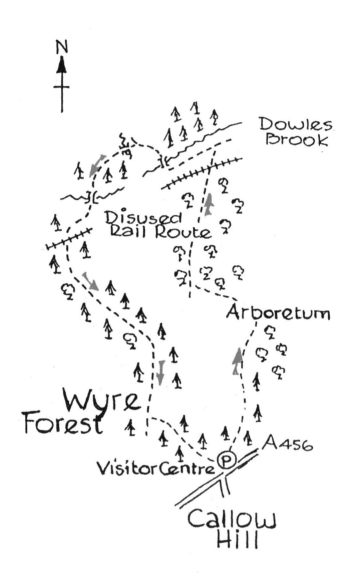

N

Dowles Brook

Disused Rail Route

Arboretum

Wyre Forest

A456

Visitor Centre Ⓟ

Callow Hill

WALK 27

right to Forhill. Go left by inn then at once right along vehicle way (Forhill House). Within half a mile climb stile on right. In field turn left. Join cart-track. Follow route past pool to join tarmac vehicle-way. Maintain direction. Just before gates to garden of house veer right. Drop to stile to fields. Continue to lane. Cross to outward path to right of house. Retrace outward route to start.

To shorten walk: Take path on left at junction of lanes on the way to Weatheroak (saves three miles).

27. *Callow Hill, Wyre Forest*

Distance of walk: 8km/5ml.
Distance from Birmingham: 38km/24ml.
Ordnance Survey maps: 138 and 952.
Refreshments: Café at visitor centre.
Paths: Good – well used and waymarked.
Terrain: Rocky tracks through woods.
Points of interest: Visitor centre indicates fauna and flora in
    Wyre Forest; old rail route through woods; Arboretum.

Wyre Forest has been designated by the Forestry Commission as a forest nature reserve. Many trees were felled from medieval times to the eighteenth century for the Bewdley shipbuilding industry. Others were used for charcoal burning.

Park in Forestry Commission carpark at Callow Hill visitor centre. 753741. Follow route marked by red rings. Cross brook along track above deep ravine. Drop down valley. At junction of tracks swing left (still following red rings) to arboretum. Bear right, now following yellow-ring route along signed public footpath to join forest 'road'. Keep on yellow-ring route to cross old rail route to wide bridleway. Turn left. Follow Dowles Brook upstream. Cross brook and keep following bridleway marked by blue arrows. Cross stream by junction of tracks – still blue-arrowed route along forest 'road'. At ford cross water using bridge. Climb out of valley. Again cross old rail route. Rejoin red-ring waymarked route near top of hill. Keep ahead and pass seats. Soon after

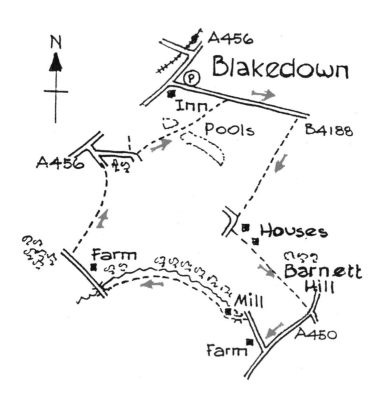

WALK 28

leave main route. Turn left along narrow path to T-junction of tracks. Turn right (red waymarks) along signed public path for half a mile to carpark.

To shorten walk: Keep on red-ring route. Saves two miles.

28. *Barnett Hill*

Distance of walk: 6.5km/4ml.
Distance from Birmingham: 25km/16ml.
Ordnance Survey maps: 139 and 953.
Refreshments: Inns, Blakedown.
Paths: Good, well-used tracks.
Terrain: Sandy soils which drain well. Route through former heathlands which now support some mixed agriculture.
Points of interest: Wildfowl on lakes; ancient mill; brooks which powered many mills and ironworks.

Barnett Hill is one of the many little hills in the undulating countryside west of the lofty Clent Hills. The locals make a good effort to keep paths open in this pleasant walking area.

Park in streets off main road (A456) in Blakedown. 880784. Walk three-quarters of a mile along B4188. By speed derestriction sign turn right along bridleway. Go over brook and through wood. Keep ahead through rough pasture to stile on lane. Turn left. Just around bend to right turn left along vehicle drive (unsigned bridleway). Climb steeply up Barnett Hill. Route goes straight through wood and drops to A450. Turn right. Take care as this is main road. Within third of a mile turn right along lane. After quarter of a mile bear left along wide vehicle-track and into woods. Cross stream – old mill nearby. Swing right to keep old building on right. Follow stream to stile to lane. Turn right. Within quarter of a mile take signed bridleway on right. The farm way goes over open arable lands. Just before main road turn right along minor road. Go past one signed bridleway on left then turn left along a second signed bridleway just after. Keep buildings on right. Track drops downhill. Keep ahead past lake to B4188. Blakedown is to left.

The walk cannot easily be shortened.

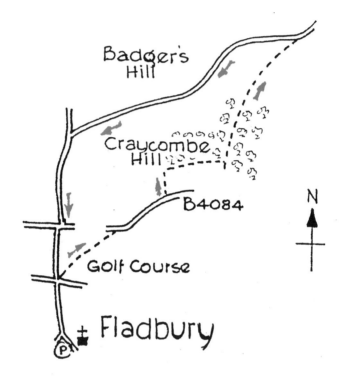

Badger's Hill

Craycombe Hill

B4084

Golf Course

N

Fladbury

WALK 29

29.   *Craycombe Hill*

Distance of walk: 8km/5ml.
Distance from Birmingham: 53km/33ml.
Ordnance Survey maps: 150 and 1019/1020.
Refreshments: Inns, Fladbury.
Paths: Not always marked on ground; part of route is Wychavon Way.
Terrain: Route climbs from the River Avon to the orchard-clothed slopes of Craycombe Hill.
Points of interest: Old mill and Norman church tower at Fladbury. Pretty stretch of river. Worcestershire novelist Francis Brett Young lived at Craycombe Manor.

Park in street at village of Fladbury. 995463. Follow main street northwards. Just over railway bridge take path signed as part of Wychavon Way on right. Path is straight and goes over golf course to stile to B4084. Turn right. After half a mile take signed path on left. Walk directly away from road to waymark post. Below Craycombe Coppice turn 90 degrees right to drive. Turn left to pass houses. Keep ahead to climb hill. Maintain direction through fields and orchards to lane. Turn left to drop down Badger's Hill. At road junction turn left to B4084 at Fladbury Cross. Go over road to lane to Fladbury.

The walk cannot be conveniently shortened.

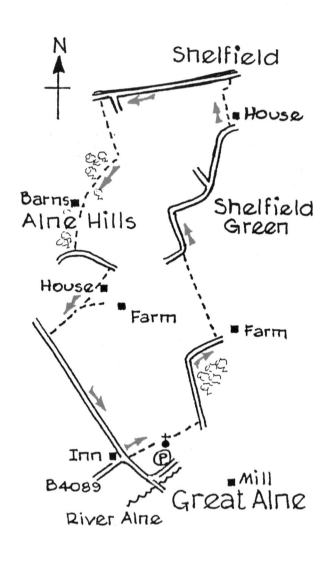

WALK 30

WARWICKSHIRE

30. *Alne Hills*

Distance of walk: 9.6km/6ml.
Distance from Birmingham: 32km/20ml.
Ordnance Survey maps: 150 and 975.
Refreshments: Inn and shop, Great Alne.
Paths: Few are clearly defined, but starts are signed.
Terrain: Gradual slopes up hills over clay soils which can cling to boots if wet.
Points of interest: Indications of old railway line (station now house). The railway (built in 1876) was called the Coffee Pot line because of unusual funnel on the engine.

These gentle heights are above the little village of Great Alne. The lanes are cut into the hillsides and have some of the beauty of quiet Devon highways.

Park in lay-by outside church gate on B4089. 118597. From the carpark take signed footpath to church. Turn right to lane. Turn left and follow lane to walk around sharp bend to right. Four hundred yards further take footpath up bank on left to stile. Keep to edge of field and stay on a constant heading at Shelfield Green. Turn right then right when the way divides. After half a mile take path by house on left. Keep ahead to stile on right. Follow waymarked path to lane. Turn left. A few steps past road junction take path on left through metal gate. Keep constant bearing to climb stile in metal gate.

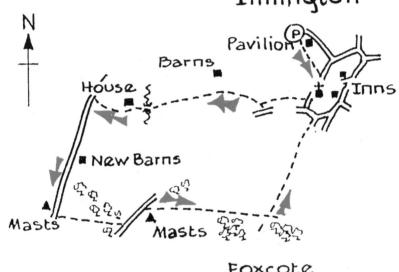

Ilmington

N

Pavilion

Barns

House

Inns

New Barns

Masts

Masts

Foxcote

WALK 31

Turn right alongside wood and enter woodlands through corner gate. Follow clear track through beech trees (which were once coppiced to provide timber for sheep hurdles). Out of woods walk along cart-track to summit of Alne Hills and continue down to road. Turn left for 300 yards. By drive to cottage take path over step-stile on right. The path leads to farm drive and road. Turn left. Opposite inn with an unusual name (Mother Huff Cap – 'huff cap' is the froth on beer) take path to church and carpark.

To shorten walk: Turn left at Shelfield Green (save three miles).

31. Ilmington Down

Distance of walk: 9km/5ml.
Distance from Birmingham: 60km/37ml.
Ordnance Survey maps: 151 and 1020.
Refreshments: Inns, Ilmington.
Paths: Good and well waymarked.
Terrain: Quite steep sections over limestone, well-drained land. Route is across pasture and along lanes.
Points of interest: Ilmington village – Norman church, manor house, old animal pound. Foxcote – eighteenth-century Palladian-style mansion.

This is the highest hill in Warwickshire at about 850ft above sea level. The upland is an outlier of the Cotswolds and therefore has the characteristics of the limestone ridge.

Park at Recreation Ground, Mickleton Road, Ilmington. 210440. From carpark cross recreation ground (with tennis courts on left) to village school. Turn right on road. By hurdlemaker's premises take cul-de-sac lane right. Keep ahead along wide track then climb at side of sheep pasture to stile to farm track. Follow wide fenced way to large hill pasture. Over ridge drop down to cross brook. Bear left over rough meadow below house to path through newly planted wood. Follow clear track which veers right to an arable field. Walk at the border to ancient drover's road. The narrow way passes newly restored barns on the left. Keep on road to top

N

Ilmington

Inns

Farm

Masts

Pool

Windmill
Hill

House

Farm

Foxcote

WALK 32

Walk 31   The Palladian-style mansion of Foxcote

of Ilmington Down. Opposite TV masts turn left. The path keeps alongside wall to corner gate to pasture. Continue to lane. Turn left then at once right along cart-track that goes by tall radio masts. Within half a mile take signed path left which drops down to Ilmington village.

To shorten walk: Leave drover's road by newly restored barns. Cut over field to high wood and follow edge to lane.

32.   *Windmill Hill Ilmington*

Distance of walk: 9km/5.5ml.
Distance from Birmingham: 60km/37ml.
Ordnance Survey maps: 151 and 1020.
Refreshments: Inns, Ilmington.
Paths: Good but not all marked on ground.
Terrain: Limestone on upland; clay in vale. Route is along lanes, through pastures and arable land.
Points of interest: Norman church and seventeenth-century manor, Ilmington; Foxcote House is eighteenth-century mansion; ancient 'green' road.

79

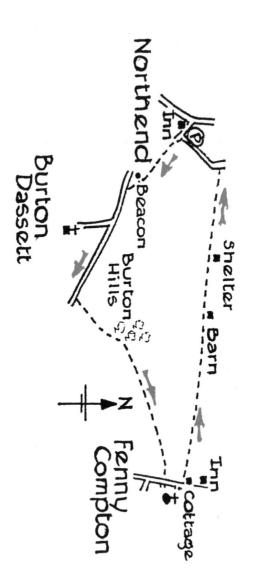

WALK 33

The windmill of the hill has long gone but there are fine views from the upland. On the way a recently built pool (where wildlife is rapidly taking hold) is passed.

Park in the street near the Red Lion Inn, Ilmington. 213435. Cross to road signed to Shipston. Past houses take lane right. Go past junction. Opposite entrance to Southfields Farm take signed path through gate right. Through further gate bear left to keep at side of reeded pool. At end bear right over rivulet to corner gate to hill pasture. Climb steep hill (badger sets on right) near left-hand border to stile to lane on Windmill Hill. Cross to drive to Foxcote. Follow main drive past front of house. Estate road dips then climbs. Once past house on right take path through gate on right. Climb field to stile. Follow path at sides of fields and woods to lane. Turn right. Within 300 yards turn right along farm road. Walk past masts and woods to lane. Cross directly over along ancient green road. Follow way of horses to lane. Turn left. Retrace steps to Ilmington.

To shorten walk: Turn right along lane on reaching Windmill Hill. Saves two-and-a-half miles.

33. *Burton Dassett Hills*

Distance of walk: 9km/6ml.
Distance from Birmingham: 51km/32ml.
Ordnance Survey maps: 151 and 1021.
Refreshments: Inns, Northend and Fenny Compton.
Paths: Some tracks not marked on the ground but way should be clear.
Terrain: The high land is of stone which drains well. The lower route is over arable fields of heavy clay which can make for heavy going in winter.
Points of interest: Magnificent upland Norman church (termed 'the Cathedral of the Hills'); stone beacon tower on hilltop; holy well outside church; Fenny Compton church with reminders of Battle of Edge Hill.

These hills now form a fine country park, established in 1971, and the area has also been designed as a site of special

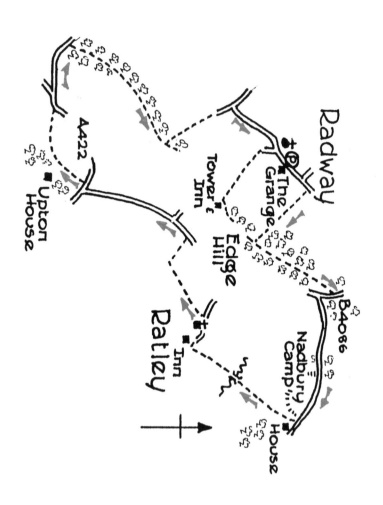

WALK 34

scientific interest. The botany and ecology have been fashioned by the now disused ironstone quarries.

Park at quiet roadsides in Northend. 391525. From main street in Northend walk along lane by inn. When lane bends keep to old direction, now going along stony track (an ancient 'road' called Mill Lane). Beyond stile climb to lane on hilltop. Turn left then right at fork to visit Burton Dassett church. Retrace steps to junction and continue right. Within third of a mile and opposite quarry entrance go through metal gate on left. Drop down hill and keep woods on left. Pick up left-hand hedges through fields. Past new barn lane is reached at Fenny Compton. Turn left and take signed path by cottage on left. Walk alongside brook then enter field. Maintain a constant heading through fields, keeping just to left of barn and animal shelter. Aim to left of distant houses. Through gates continue along vehicle drive at back of houses to road. Turn left to Northend.

The walk cannot conveniently be shortened.

34. *Edge Hill*

Distance of walk: 13km/8ml.
Distance from Birmingham: 69km/43ml.
Ordnance Survey maps: 151 and 1021.
Refreshments: Inns, Edgehill and Ratley.
Paths: Some are not marked on the ground and not well walked.
Terrain: The route is over sown fields (clay soils), pastureland and through high woods.
Points of interest: Seventeenth-century Upton House (NT); The Grange – owned by the Washingtons (family of US president); tower where King's standard was raised; Nadbury Bronze Age earthwork; thirteenth-century church, Ratley.

On 23 October 1642 the Battle of Edge Hill – the first skirmish of the Civil War – was fought here. The site of the fighting is inaccessible (War Dept land to N of ridge). The King's troops camped on Edge Hill – a tower marks the place.

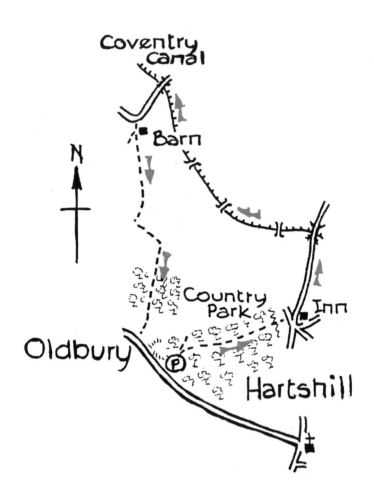

WALK 35

Park at quiet roadsides in Radway. 368481. From church walk through village. After quarter of a mile turn right along second drive by Grafton Cottage. Continue to meadow. Keep ahead to enter woods and junction of tracks. Turn left to road. Turn right and left along B4086 at junction. After three-quarters of a mile (just before farm) turn right through gate. Drop down valley; keep direction climbing hill. Swing around house to right. Follow vehicle-way to Ratley. Walk past church to farm drive on left. Here path starts. Route marked by stiles to cart-track. Go right to road. Turn left then right at A422. Just past Upton House is farm drive and path. Climb fence. Walk to far end of pasture. Bear right to join cart-track to main road. Turn left for quarter of a mile. Opposite farm drive turn right along unsigned path through woods. Follow waymark arrows. At tarmac vehicle drive keep ahead. At bridleway turn left to lane. Turn right to Radway.

To shorten walk: At first junction of paths in woods turn right to Tower inn. Drop down steps to Radway – saves six-and-a-half miles.

35. Hartshill

Distance of walk: 8km/5ml.
Distance from Birmingham: 32km/20ml.
Ordnance Survey maps: 140 and 914.
Refreshments: Café, country park; Inn, Hartshill.
Paths: Fieldpaths are well used and clear; towpath alongside
   Coventry Canal.
Terrain: Well-drained soils; these are sandy in the extensive
   woods but there are quarries for roadstone in the area.
Points of interest: Visitor centre at country park with
   interesting exhibits; waymarked trails through woods;
   Coventry Canal dates from 1780; site of Iron Age camp;
   memorial to sixteenth-century poet, Michael Drayton.

Hartshill was not a hill where stags roamed but was the Saxon Heardred's Hill in the Kingdom of Mercia. A strategic hill-fort was built in the Iron Age. The area was once part of

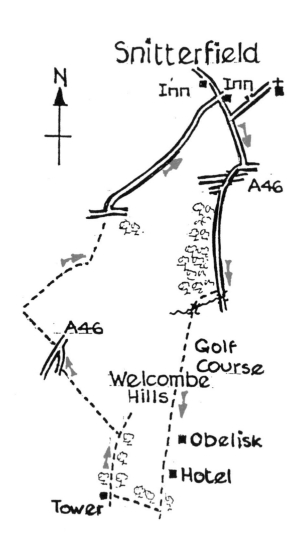

WALK 36

the vast Forest of Arden and was well wooded at the time of the Domesday Survey. Much was replanted with lime trees towards the end of the eighteenth century. These were coppiced to provide blocks for the hatters of Atherstone.

Park at carpark in Hartshill Country Park. 317943. From visitor centre walk through barrier to woods. Stay on main track to waymark post (numbered two). Keep on arrowed way (posts three and four). At post four keep ahead uphill through trees. Emerging from trees, walk along path to road at Hartshill. Turn right then left. (Drayton memorial – opened by John Betjeman in 1972 – is nearby.) Drop down Atherstone Road to canal. Gain towpath and walk with water on left. At first road bridge leave canal. Turn left on road to cross water. Within 300 yards keep ahead when road turns right. Once past barn turn left along signed path. Follow clear path over hill to quarry notice. Turn left and follow clear path to woods. Turn left and climb hill to grassed area. (Hill-fort is away to right.) On lane turn left to carpark.

The walk cannot be conveniently shortened.

36. Welcombe Hills, Stratford-upon-Avon

Distance of walk: 11km/7ml.
Distance from Birmingham: 35km/22ml.
Ordnance Survey maps: 151, SP 05/15 and SP 25/35.
Refreshments: Inns, Snitterfield.
Paths: Most of the paths are well used.
Terrain: Part of route is along quiet lanes; the Welcombe Hills are of park woods and pasture.
Points of interest: Clopton folly tower, 120ft-high obelisk erected in 1876 in memory of Mark Philips; Welcombe Hall (Victorian mansion of 1867 built by Manchester manufacturer); St James's fifteenth-century church, Snitterfield; barn said to have been home of Richard Shakespeare (William's grandfather).

These hills (now a country park) were obtained for the town of Stratford-upon-Avon through the generosity of the Flowers family. The Flowers were brewers who were great

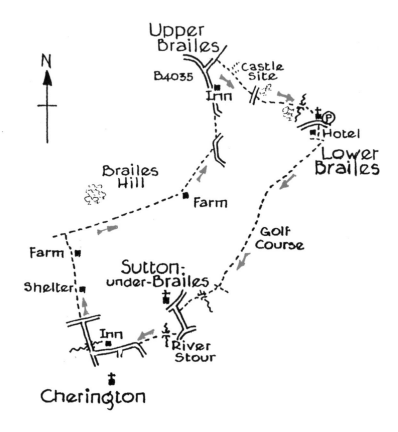

WALK 37

benefactors to the theatre and many other projects. The lands were originally the grounds of the magnificent Welcombe Hall – once a stately home but now a hotel.

Park at quiet roadsides in Snitterfield. From church walk along road to T-junction. Turn left then right by war memorial. Cross new bypass. (The old road here was King's Lane along which Charles II escaped after Battle of Worcester.) Keep ahead when lane divides. After one mile look for start of hidden footpath on right 30 yards before railing bridge. Beyond rough ground cross over a footbridge to new golf course. Waymarks and stiles show the way to Welcombe Hills Country Park. Continue alongside left-hand wall surrounding hotel to stile to woods. At division of paths fork left to pasture. Turn right (woods on right) to Clopton Tower. Turn right over stile and keep ahead to waymarked bridleway to lane. Turn right to main road. Cross to path through kissing gate opposite. Walk alongside left-hand hedge for 400 yards then turn 90 degrees right to walk over field to opposite boundary. Pick up line of ditch (on left). Go over bridge and keep on same direction to lane. Cross to opposite lane to Snitterfield.

To shorten walk: Turn right at obelisk to main road (saves one mile).

37. Brailes Hill

Distance of walk: 13km/8ml.
Distance from Birmingham: 62km/39ml.
Ordnance Survey maps: 151 and 1044.
Refreshments: Inns, hotels, Upper and Lower Brailes and Cherington.
Paths: Tracks signed on road; some not marked on ground.
Terrain: Arable and pasture land; lowland paths can be muddy.
Points of interest: Norman church (parts eleventh century) 'The Cathedral of the Feldon'; castle site; Cherington's church tower is fifteenth century.

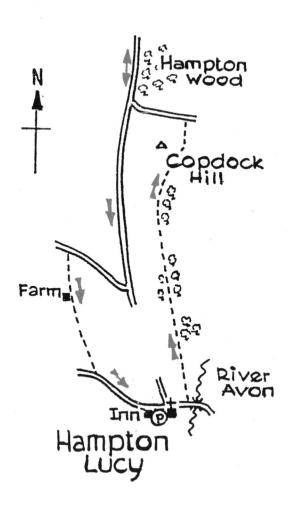

N

Hampton Wood

Copdock Hill

Farm

River Avon

Inn

Hampton Lucy

WALK 38

On top of Brailes Hill – the second highest point in Warks – is a group of trees (Highwall Coppice), but to locals this is Brailes Clump. No right of way to summit but footpath climbs to some height. Much of hill is arable; in medieval times Brailes was the third largest town in the country (its wealth founded on sheep).

Park at roadside by Brailes church. 310392. From church cross B4035 and follow pathway to left of inn. At junction of paths take way left to meadows. Turn right. Keep brook on right through golf course to bold farm track. Cross to field opposite then at once cross bridge. Follow arrowed path to lane. Turn left and keep ahead at junction. Within a few steps take path on right. The path goes over River Stour then through pastures (where ridges and hollows mark site of moated manor house) to lane. Keep ahead past inn at Cherington. (There is path nearby over field to church.) Turn right at T-junction. At next junction keep ahead to path. Climb field past animal shelter. Keep ruined farmhouse on right to bridleway. Turn right. The way passes a farm below summit of Brailes Hill to lane. Turn left for 400 yards to path on left to road. Turn left then right at junction. Take footpath on right between houses. Continue to right of castle knoll to lane. Cross to opposite path. Over stream aim to right of farm to Brailes church.

To shorten walk: After descending to lane after Brailes Hill keep along lane to Lower Brailes – saves one mile.

38.   Copdock Hill

Distance of walk: 9km/6ml.
Distance from Birmingham: 42km/26ml.
Ordnance Survey maps: 151 and 998.
Refreshments: Inn, Hampton Lucy.
Paths: Some are not marked on ground but there are no route-finding problems.
Terrain: The route is along paths over arable fields and through woods which can be heavy going if wet. There is some lane walking.

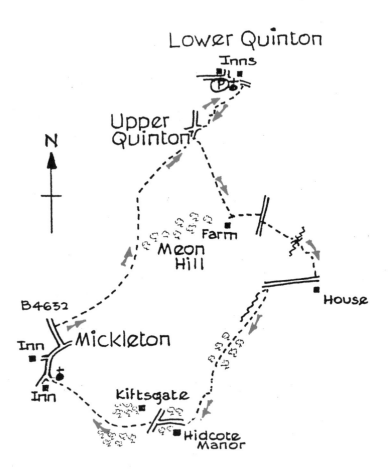

WALK 39

Points of interest: Charlecote House and deer (with Shakespeare associations); restored water mill at Charlecote; Hampton parish church built in Gothic style; Hampton Wood – old preserved woodlands in care of Nature Trust; Hampton bridge is one of oldest cast-iron bridges in country.

This little hill rises only to about 300ft but the gentle climb gives views over the River Avon and the parkland of the Elizabethan National Trust house of Charlecote. 'Copdock' means 'copped oak' or 'an oak tree rising to a top'.

Park at quiet roadside in Hampton Lucy. 257571. By Hampton Lucy's bridge over Avon walk along vehicle-track. After 100 yards go through gate and turn left, following bridleway signs (blue arrows). Walk through wood then go at sides of arable fields. There is another gate and path through second wood. Pass through gateway on summit of Copdock Hill. Cross open field following line of trees. At opposite hedge turn right then left through hedge gap. Regain old direction to lane. Turn left then right at T-junction to Hampton Wood. Retrace steps along lane and continue for one-and-a-half miles. Turn right. After half a mile turn left down farm drive. The path goes to left of house then at borders of fields to road. Hampton Lucy is left.

To shorten walk: Omit Hampton Wood and turn left at T-junction saving two miles.

39. Meon Hill

Distance of walk: 13km/8ml.
Distance from Birmingham: 50km/31ml.
Ordnance Survey maps: 151 and 1020.
Refreshments: Inns, Lower Quinton and Mickleton.
Paths: Many tracks not marked on ground but ways are clear.
  Route includes Heart of England Way and Centenary Way.
Points of interest: Village of Quinton belonged to Magdalen
  College (see coat of arms on inn); fine churches with tall
  spires and Norman work at Quinton and Mickleton; lovely
  gardens at Hidcote (National Trust) and Kiftsgate.

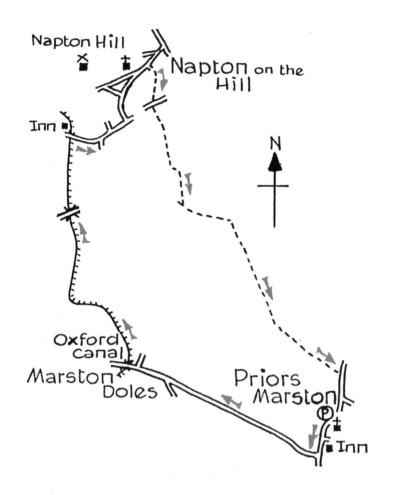

Napton Hill

Napton on the Hill

N

Inn

Oxford canal

Marston Doles

Priors Marston

Inn

WALK 40

Meon Hill is like a miniature flat-topped Table Mountain. It is an outlier of the Cotswolds and capped by ridges of an Iron Age fort. Folklore tales abound but the hill became notorious when a farm labourer was found dead on the slopes on St Valentine's Day in 1945, killed with his own pitchfork. The mystery remains unsolved.

Park at quiet roadside by church in Lower Quinton. 178472. By churchyard footpath is signed; follow unmarked path through fields to farm track. Turn right to lane at Upper Quinton. Turn left then bear left at green. Within few hundred yards take footpath signed by Meon Cottage on left. Follow waymarked path of Centenary Way over fields to farm drive. Turn left then right on lane. Within a few steps continue on Centenary Way over stile left. Follow waymarked route to road by house. Turn right for 400 yards to signed path over stile left. Follow brook then climb hill to carpark. Gain cul-de-sac lane to road junction by Kiftsgate. Go through gateway and follow signed track which drops steeply down hillside. Follow arrowed way to Mickleton. On B4632 turn right and follow road round sharp bend. Within 200 yards take path down vehicle-drive on right. Path is waymarked to Upper Quinton; retrace steps to Lower Quinton.

To shorten walk: Turn right on first lane after Upper Quinton. Follow lanes to Mickleton – saves two miles.

40.   *Napton on the Hill*

Distance of walk: 14km/9ml.
Distance from Birmingham: 54km/34ml.
Ordnance Survey maps: 151, 999 and 977.
Refreshments: Inns, Priors Marston and Napton.
Paths: Some are little used and difficult across fields.
Terrain: Pastoral and arable lowlands; towpaths and lanes.
Points of interest: Napton windmill and church; Oxford Canal (opened 1790) with locks; ancient 'salt way'; thirteenth-century church Priors Marston.

Two fine buildings crown this hill which rises 500ft (158m) above the plain where the Oxford Canal twists a tortuous

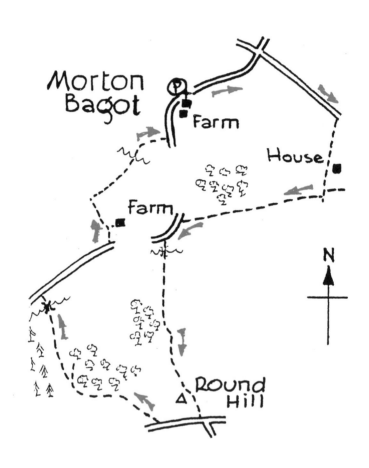

Morton Bagot

Farm

House

Farm

N

Round Hill

WALK 41

route. There is a windmill (of which records go back to 1543) and the twelfth-century St Lawrence Church.

Park at quiet roadside in Priors Marston. 489576. At Priors Marston war memorial take lane signed to Southam. Climb to ridgetop then drop down to canal. Follow towpath northwards to bridge no. 113. Walk along lanes to Napton and climb to hilltop. Descend lane to main street. Turn right then left down track. Keep ahead to road. Turn right and at once left down farm track. Cross brook and go through metal gate. Keep alongside hedges. After another metal gate turn left (left-hand hedge). In next pasture turn sharp right past pond. Through bridle gate keep at side of field to metal gate to bridleway. Turn left through gate. Climb rise beside hedge and walk through gateway (no gate). Pass through hunting gate. Walk by hedge to gap to open field. Veer right to diagonal corner. Pass through new gate to right of barn. Keep heading to cross field to gate to next field (often arable). Follow right-hand border and around corner left. At next corner turn 90 degrees right through hedge gap along wide bridleway to lane. Turn right to village.

This walk cannot be shortened.

41.   *Round Hill, Morton Bagot*

Distance of walk: 9km/6ml.
Distance from Birmingham: 30km/19ml.
Ordnance Survey maps: 150 and 975.
Refreshments: Should be carried.
Paths: Mostly good tracks but unmarked and poor near end of route. Part of route along Heart of England Way.
Terrain: Mixture of woods, pasture and arable land.
Points of interest: Little Norman church, Morton Bagot; Church Farm with large timber-framed barn; woodland nature reserve.

Round Hill is a little knoll in some fine, albeit unspectacular, undulating countryside. The area is remote although not far from large towns.

Park at roadside in Morton Bagot. 112648. Walk eastwards away from church along lane. At crossroads turn right. After

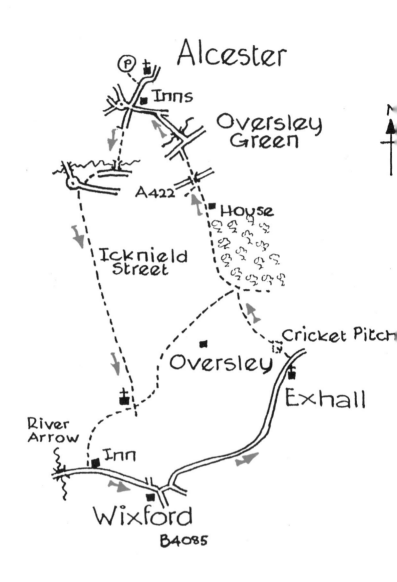

WALK 42

half a mile take unsigned path through metal gate on right. Walk beside left-hand hedge. Go past house; just beyond go through gate to join house drive. Take signed bridleway to right along 'green' road then ahead over open field to join Heart of England Way. Go through hunting gate; walk at borders of fields and along grassy track to lane. Turn left. At once go through gate left. Drop down to bridge over brook and through bushes to rough pasture. Follow waymarked route over fields to gate by corner of woods. Follow route around to left of Round Hill and over stiles to lane. Turn right. A few yards down hill take hidden path up bank right. In top field walk to stile towards woods then through hunting gate to woods. Turn left along vehicle-track. When track enters woods go through gate left. Walk through large field to far end. Go through rough metal gate and over plank bridge. Keep ahead to lane. Turn right. After half a mile turn left down drive of Netherstead Farm. As drive bends right to farmhouse keep ahead beside little left-hand wood and barns to field. Walk to far border. Turn right to corner fence-stile. Keep by wire fence to corner gate then another right. Cut off corner of field to fence-stile under willow tree. Go diagonally over pasture and cross brook (no bridge). Keep direction through meadow to gate. In arable field walk at edge of lane. Turn left to Morton Bagot.

To shorten walk: Turn right on early lane – saves three miles.

42. *Oversley Hill*

Distance of walk: 9km/6ml.
Distance from Birmingham: 30km/19ml.
Ordnance Survey maps: 150 and 997.
Refreshments: Inns and cafés, Alcester, inns, Wixford.
Paths: Good, well-used tracks.
Terrain: Lowland paths at start are over clay soils; later route climbs and borders woodlands.
Points of interest: Alcester was Roman town; fourteenth-century church; town hall built in 1618; Icknield Street, Roman road; Wixford church has finest brasses in county; 400-year-old bridge.

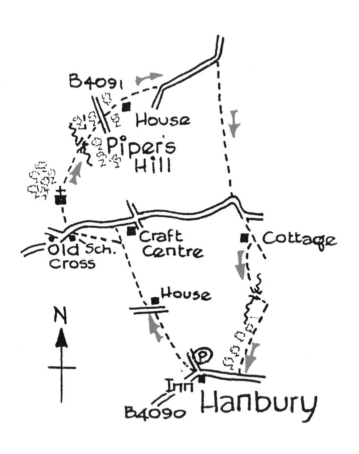

WALK 43

The walk starts along Icknield Street to Wixford. Quiet lanes lead to Exhall village and the climb up Oversley Hill to fine woodlands. We have views of Oversley Castle (not designed for battle but as a house).

Park in carpark off High Street. Walk along the main street from the church to cross the Stratford Road. 909573. Continue down Bleachfield Street. Keep ahead to cross River Arrow to lane. Turn right. Lane becomes bridleway to cross A422. This is now Icknield Street. Keep ahead to Wixford church. Turn right (church on right). Follow path to B4035 by inn. Turn left. Take second lane left opposite inn. When lane divides take left-hand way to Exhall. Just past church take signed path left. Cross cricket pitch to step-stile to sheep pastures. Continue climbing up Oversley Hill to stile to arable field. Continue to junction of tracks. Turn left and keep at side of right-hand dense woods. The track joins a house drive; go over main road to T-junction at Oversley Green. Turn right then left. Cross old bridge to Alcester.

To shorten walk: Take path left by Wixford church. Saves one mile.

43. Piper's Hill

Distance of walk: 8km/5ml.
Distance from Birmingham: 32km/20ml.
Ordnance Survey maps: 150 and 974.
Refreshments: Inn, Hanbury; restaurant, Jinny Ring craft
    centre.
Paths: Poor and ill-defined at start of walk.
Terrain: Good, well-drained soils; route is over pastures,
    through woodlands and along lanes and cart-tracks.
Points of interest: Beech-woods; stump of ancient cross;
    Hanbury church with thirteenth-century work; locals like
    to think Ambridge (village in *The Archers*) is based on
    Hanbury; Jinny Ring centre (country craftsmen at work).

Piper's Hill is a wooded knoll astride the B4091 and the beauty of the beech trees in autumn should dictate when this walk is tackled. It is one of the few remnants of the once-vast

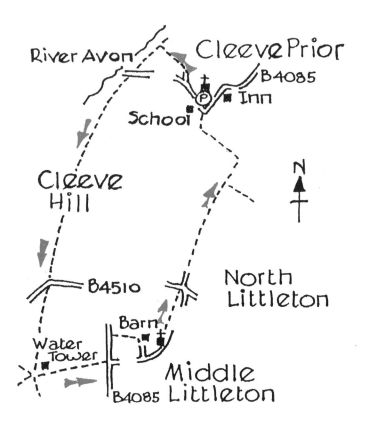

WALK 44

Forest of Feckenham which surrounded over 60 villages and hamlets in its 200 square miles. As it was a royal forest, there were strict laws on poaching and taking of wood.

Park off main road. 966630. Opposite Vernon Arms Inn take path signed alongside garden of house (through gate by garage). Keep ahead at side of garden and fields to cross farm track. Bear slightly right. Walk over open field, aiming towards house with dormer windows. Climb stile to lane and turn left for 100 yards. Turn right at signed path. Cross meadow to metal gate to next field. Walk at right-hand borders of fields to newly planted wood. Halfway along climb stile left. Walk to distant school. On lane cross to opposite signed path. Climb hill to church. In far corner of churchyard go through kissing gate. Drop down hill and cross brook then enter wood at Piper's Hill. Cross B4091 and walk through woods to far border. Pick up path along vehicle-way then to left of house. Continue to lane. As lane twists left go right along cart-track to road. Stay on road for 200 yards. Walk along farm drive to path just beyond cottage. In pasture go at right-hand border then left side of next fields. At far corner climb stile left and cross brook. Climb hill by left-hand hedge then wood. Follow signed path to road. Hanbury is on right.

To shorten walk: At newly planted wood keep ahead to lane. Turn right to Jinny Ring craft centre. Cross to opposite lane. Saves three miles.

44. *Cleeve Hill, Cleeve Prior*

Distance of walk: 11km/7ml.
Distance from Birmingham: 40km/25ml.
Ordnance Survey maps: 150 and 1020.
Refreshments: Inn, Cleeve Prior.
Paths: Some not marked on ground.
Terrain: Walk over arable land – much given over to market gardens.
Points of interest: Cleeve Manor (hiding place for friends of Charles I); Cleeve church has fifteenth-century tower; Littleton thirteenth-century tithe barn (NT).

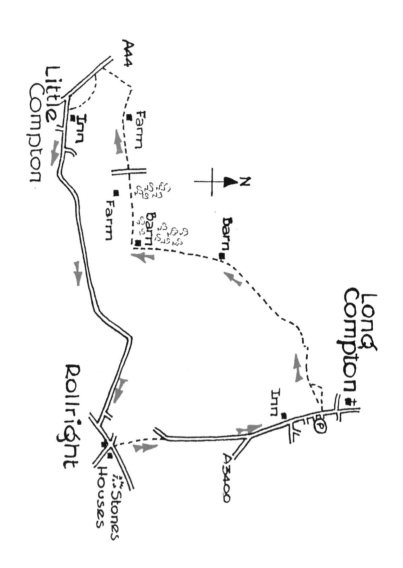

WALK 45

Cleeve Hill is a rocky ridge running 200ft above the River Avon. Quarries provided hard, grey stone for the old buildings (manor, church, forge, cider mill, inn, weaver's barn, etc.) of Cleeve Prior.

Park in street near church. 087492. Walk along B4085. Turn right (signed West End). Keep ahead along Nightingale Lane to signed footpath to River Avon. At vehicle-way above river turn left to lane. Cross to opposite track (bridleway) by nature reserve. At road cross to bridleway and proceed to stile. Climb stile and walk along path. At division keep left. Pass water trough and continue on same heading at double stile. At further stile bear left to join main track by water tower. At junction of tracks take wide way left to road. Turn left to signed path over stile right to tithe barn. Take road to church. In corner of churchyard go through metal kissing gate. Keep to right of church to gate to garden. Keep ahead to step-stile then another. Bear slightly right over field alongside right-hand fence to lane (to right of cottage) near junction. Walk along W side. At bend of lane keep ahead along signed bridleway. Walk at sides of fields to meeting of tracks. Turn right over brook. Regain old direction to farm road to Cleeve Prior.

The route cannot be shortened.

45. Rollright

Distance of walk: 9km/6ml.
Distance from Birmingham: 64km/40ml.
Ordnance Survey maps: 151 and 1044.
Refreshments: Inns, Long Compton and Little Compton.
Paths: Good paths – not always defined on ground.
Terrain: Limestone soils which drain well; these are sheep-rearing hills, with steep sharp slopes.
Points of interest: Rollright Stones – stones (circle and groups) set in place for ritual purposes during Bronze Age (1500BC). Long Compton – ancient village cross; Norman church (400-year-old lych gate). Little Compton – manor house; 600-year-old church tower.

The ridge climbed on the walk overlooks the valley of the River Stour with fine views of the Cotswolds.

Park in street off main road. 287327. Next to village shop and pump (village cross) walk along farm drive. Keep on the main track, passing through gates and by barns. Track goes to left of woods to meeting of tracks by barn. Turn right along clear track. Join farm drive and continue to a road. Cross directly over to farm track opposite. This is a bridleway and goes by a farm. Proceed to A44. Turn left. Within 200 yards take path on left to Little Compton. Continue along lane to T-junction. Turn left and walk through village. Keep ahead at junctions to T-junction. Turn left. Near next crossroads are ancient stones. Retrace steps to crossroads. Turn right along footpath. Join lane. Turn right to pass farms to A3400 and Long Compton.

To shorten walk: Turn left at first lane on walk – saves one-and-a-half miles.

Walk 45   The King Stone

106

Walk 51   The walk starts at Stanton – a lovely Cotswold village

*Walk 52   Dover's Hill. The Olympic Games were run
along the ridge*

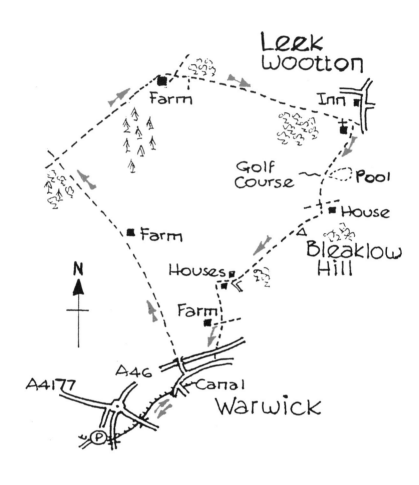

WALK 46

46. *Bleaklow Hill*

Distance of walk: 11km/7ml.
Distance from Birmingham: 33.5km/21ml.
Ordnance Survey maps: 151 and 976.
Refreshments: Inn, Leek Wootton.
Paths: Farm 'roads' used; some paths not often walked but way clear and waymarked.
Terrain: Farmland – pastoral and arable. Caution required where new golf course constructed – paths may be diverted.
Points of interest: Grand Union Canal; Goodrest Farm (historic site where Queen Elizabeth stayed); Leek Wootton church – fifteenth-century tower; Gaveston's Cross.

It was on Bleaklow Hill that Piers Gaveston (Edward II's favourite) was beheaded by the barons in 1313. There is a monument marking the spot (not on public land).

Park at carpark entered from lane near roundabout junction of A4177 and A46 W of Warwick. 267655. Carpark by canal. Cross water at lock and turn right along towpath. By cemetery go along vehicle drive to road. Turn left. Within third of a mile bear left along private farm road (public bridleway). At crossroads of 'roads' by wood after one-and-a-half miles turn right to farmstead. Follow signed path around farm to drive. Cross to opposite path. Walk over field towards woods. Keep woods on left. Continue at sides of fields to Leek Wootton. Keep ahead along path to church. Walk through churchyard along avenue of low trees to house drive. Cross to opposite path to field. Keep heading over further drive. Drop down hill to new golf course. Maintain heading on waymarked route by new lake. Climb out of valley to vehicle drive. Cross and walk at edge of field for few steps. Turn right. (Trig point of Bleaklow Hill on left.) Continue to vehicle drive by houses. Keep on drive a few steps. As drive swings left take path ahead. Go around house (keep on left) and take signed path over field to farm drive. Bearing right take path to stile (house away to right) on to A46. Cross road to opposite stile. Follow path to estate road.

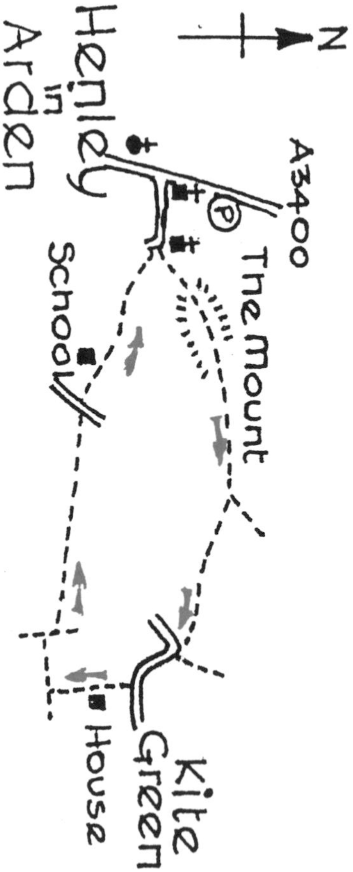

N

A3400

Henley
in
Arden

School

The Mount

Kite
Green

House

WALK 47

Continue to main road. Turn right. Retrace steps by canal to start.

The walk cannot easily be shortened.

47.   The Mount – Henley-in-Arden

Distance of walk: 5km/3ml.
Distance from Birmingham: 28km/15ml.
Ordnance Survey maps: 151 and 975.
Refreshments: Inns and tea-rooms, Henley-in-Arden.
Paths: Clear paths but not all marked on ground.
Terrain: mixed arable and pastoral farmland
Points of interest: Fifteenth-century Henley church; Norman
    Beaudesert church; pretty buildings in Henley High Street.

The short walk is over the hill called The Mount. This strategic viewpoint was the site of the great castle built by the de Montforts. No trace of castle remains except earthworks.

Streetside parking in High Street, Henley-in-Arden. 152660. Go down Beaudesert Lane. Cross river. Keep ahead through gate by Beaudesert church. Climb steep hill. Keep ahead along ridge to climb distant hill to junction of paths. Take path over stile right. In meadow follow line of electricity cable to stile to lane. Turn left. Go around bend. Within few hundred yards lane twists sharp left. Take path signed by house. Keep ahead alongside garden and climb stiles to meadow. Keep ahead. Halfway over field turn 90 degrees right. Walk down middle of field to stile to track. Turn right for few steps. Climb stile left to field. Keep at border to lane. Cross over to field. Keep direction at edge. In corner climb stile. Path drops down bank to estate road. Follow path by school to Beaudesert Lane to return to Henley.

This walk is short and does not merit shortening.

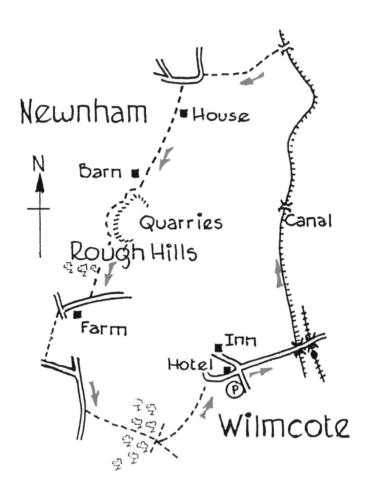

Newnham

House

Barn

Quarries

Rough Hills

Farm

Canal

Inn

Hotel

P

Wilmcote

N

WALK 48

48. Rough Hills

Distance of walk: 9km/6ml.
Distance from Birmingham: 35km/22ml.
Ordnance Survey maps: 151 and 997.
Refreshments: Inns, Wilmcote.
Paths: Towpath of canal; other parts not often marked on ground but way is clear.
Terrain: Outward route alongside canal; route through arable and pastoral farmland; some tracks can be muddy at times.
Points of interest: House of Shakespeare's mother (Mary Arden); museum of agricultural machinery; Stratford Canal (built early nineteenth century).

The Rough Hills are a modest height along a ridge of a hard rock called blue lias. This was extensively quarried in the nineteenth century and gave employment to over 50 per cent of the local population. Some of the stone was used at the Palace of Westminster.

Park in the street at Wilmcote (three miles north of Stratford-on-Avon). 164580. Walk along lane to canal. Gain towing path. Walk northwards. At second bridge after one-and-a-half miles cross water to field. Walk at edge to far gate. Through this walk over pasture to stile to lane at Newnham. Turn left. Just before green turn left down vehicle drive. Follow past house and barn. Keep ahead, gradually climbing Rough Hills. Old quarries on left. Walk around edges of fields (left-hand borders) to far step-stile by gate and woods. Drop down off Rough Hills through field to lane. Turn right to junction. Cross to opposite field. Walk alongside right-hand hedge to lane. Left to junction then right. Within quarter of a mile take signed bridleway left. Follow wide track to woods. Follow blue arrows to climb ridge. Go through gate to field. Leave waymarked bridleway. Bear left to climb stile at top of hill. Walk by fence. Climb stile to horse gallops. Turn right to Wilmcote.

To shorten walk: On lane after Rough Hills turn left to Wilmcote. Saves one mile.

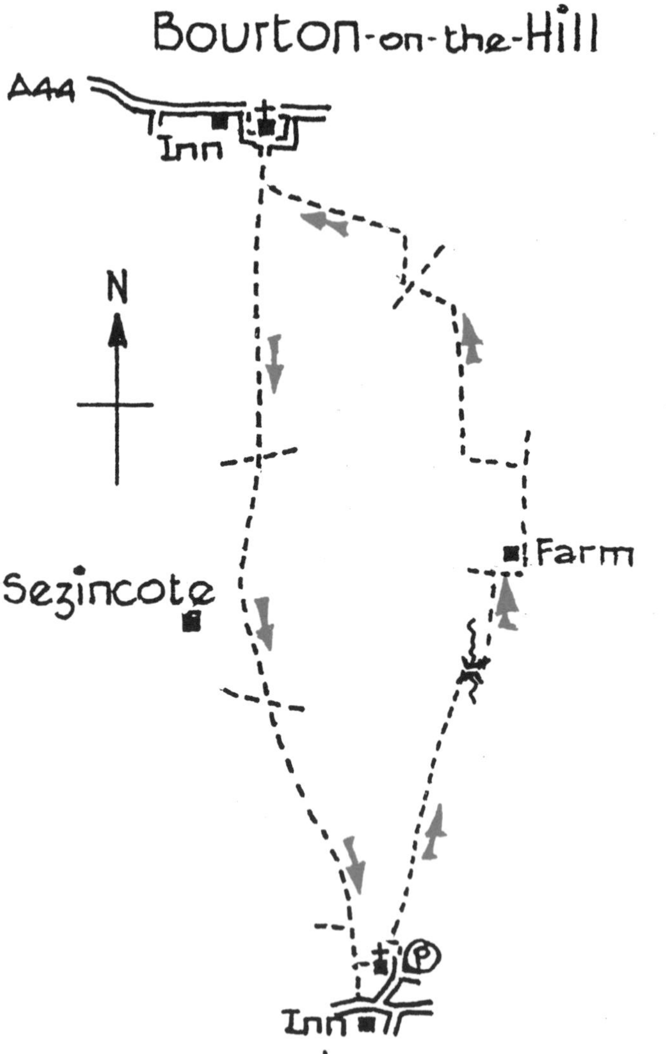

Bourton-on-the-Hill

A44

Inn

N

Sezincote

Farm

Inn

Longborough

WALK 49

GLOUCESTERSHIRE

49. *Bourton-on-the-Hill*

Distance of walk: 8km/5ml.
Distance from Birmingham: 75km/47ml.
Ordnance Survey maps: 151, 163 and 1043.
Refreshments: Inns, Longborough and Bourton-on-the-Hill.
Paths: Clear, waymarked tracks.
Terrain: Route through parkland and over meadows and arable fields.
Points of interest: Norman church and tithe barn, Bourton; Sezincote; Longborough church has 700-year-old tower; pretty Cotswold stone villages.

On the return path the route passes a spectacular house; 'Sezincote', built in 1805, has oriental 'onion' domes and was featured by John Betjeman in his autobiographical poem 'Summoned by Bells'.

At 650 feet, Bourton-on-the-Hill lies on a hillside 200 feet below the summit of this hill.

Park at roadside in Longborough. 179297. From Longborough village take lane opposite inn. Past church bear left along road to farm. Maintain heading past barns and through farmyard. Climb stile and continue through pastures to pick up right-hand ditch to pass into adjoining field over bridge. Regain former direction (left-hand hedge) to bridge over stream. Continue to farm. Turn right to farm drive. Through gate turn left. Along vehicle-way keep farmhouse

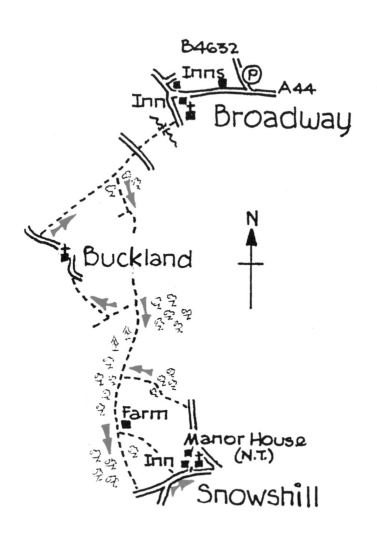

WALK 50

on left. Look for stile left (waymarked). In field walk by hedge (on left side) to bridge. Follow by wire fence and brook to wood and track to meadow. Continue to corner-stile. Go over farm track then follow arrowed way around fields to junction of paths. Turn right. This way leads to Bourton-on-the-Hill. Retrace steps to junction of paths. Keep ahead. Follow waymarks through fields (Sezincote away to right). Cross drive. Keep ahead through parkland. Go over brook to signed meeting of paths. Still maintain direction through fields to Longborough.

The walk cannot be shortened.

50. *Snowshill*

Distance of walk: 13km/8ml.
Distance from Birmingham: 58km/36ml.
Ordnance Survey maps: 150 and 1043.
Refreshments: Inns and tea-rooms, Broadway; inn, Snowshill.
Paths: Good, well-walked tracks; part of route along Cotswold Way.
Terrain: Limestone countryside; mixture of rough pasture, woods and farm tracks.
Points of interest: Broadway's main street; 1840 church was built because old church was a mile distant; Snowshill Manor House; Buckland church (600-year-old tower) has unique tapestry pall.

In past centuries villages were sited in sheltered valleys; Snowshill is unusual in that it is perched high on the Cotswolds. The garden of the inn has a splendid view straight down the valley and alongside is Snowshill Manor House. The house is owned by the National Trust and contains an eccentric collection of objects from around the world.

Park at Broadway carpark off B4632. 100376. From carpark walk along A44. Turn left along lane signed Snowshill. Opposite church take signed path (Cotswold Way). The path is clear over brook and fields to lane. Cross to opposite path and climb hill to wood. Follow Cotswold

117

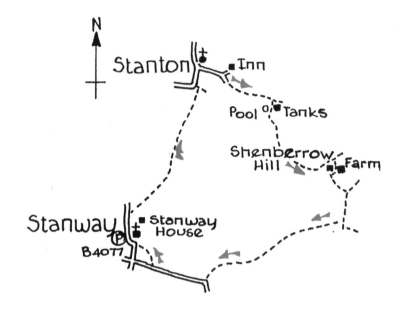

WALK 51

Way waymarks through wood and to cart-track by sheds. Maintain heading. Within half a mile Cotswold Way twists right. Keep old heading and remain on vehicle-way through a gate and to lane at Snowshill. Turn left to village. Walk past inn and Manor House. Look for path over stile on left by house drive. Take arrowed direction over fields to wood. Follow path to sheep pasture. Climb hill alongside left-hand wall. Go over ladder-stile to outward vehicle-track. Turn right to Cotswold Way route at junction of tracks. Turn left. Stay on track for 400 yards. Climb stile right. Follow waymarked route to Buckland. Walk along road past church. Take path on right over fields to Broadway.

To shorten walk: Take path near inn at Snowshill. Walk over fields to outward vehicle way. Retrace steps to Cotswold Way route at junction of tracks. Saves one mile.

51. Shenberrow Hill

Distance of walk: 8km/5ml.
Distance from Birmingham: 59km/37ml.
Ordnance Survey maps: 150 and 1043.
Refreshments: Inn, Stanton.
Paths: Good paths extensively waymarked by Cotswold wardens. Part of walk is on Cotswold Way.
Terrain: Uplands are of limestone which drains well. Route is along rough hill pastures, meadows and woodlands.
Points of interest: Stanway House, spacious seventeenth-century mansion; Stanway and Stanton churches are both Norman; fifteenth-century tithe barn at Stanway; Stanton medieval stone cross; Shenberrow fort; pretty Cotswold villages.

The wooded hill ('shen' means beautiful) rises to over 900ft and this defensive strategic height was used by the Ancient Britons to build a vast fort which covered three acres. The construction was multi-vallate with a complex plan of ditches and ramparts which can be seen today.

Park at quiet roadside in Stanway. 061323. From church at Stanway walk along lane away from main road. Within few

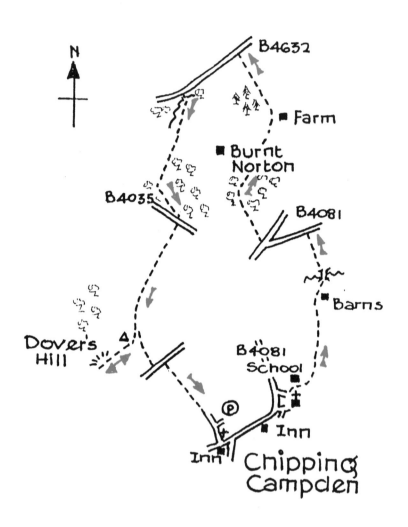

WALK 52

hundred yards path is signed on right. Follow Cotswold Way waymarks over fields to Stanton. Walk along main road, passing near church and village cross. When road divides take right fork signed as no-through road. (Inn along left fork.) At end of road continue along vehicle-way (signed as footpath). By water tanks bear right off main track over step-stile. Follow waymarked route to right then regain old heading, climbing to farmhouse. Pass through metal gate to left of house and continue to signed junction of tracks. Turn right and bear right through farmyard to another signed junction of tracks. Turn left (signed as bridleway). Walk by right-hand stone wall to pass through gate and turn right. Within 400 yards turn right to follow waymarked bridleway which follows clear track through woodlands to B4077. Turn right down hill. After half a mile take path right over field to Stanway.

The walk cannot conveniently be shortened.

52. *Dover's Hill*

Distance of walk: 11km/7ml.
Distance from Birmingham: 59km/37ml.
Ordnance Survey maps: 151 and 1043.
Refreshments: Inns, tea-rooms, Chipping Campden.
Paths: Well-trodden tracks, usually signed on road. Many
    waymarked. Part of route is Cotswold Way.
Terrain: Soils are clay in lower lands; upper route is over
    well-drained meadows.
Points of interest: Chipping Campden (wealthy 'wool town'
    in medieval times) has many fascinating buildings: church
    with 120ft tower built by wool merchants in fifteenth
    century; old market hall (1627) (NT); former grammar
    school (1628); Woolstapler's Hall (now museum of
    curios); gateway of Campden House (set on fire in Civil
    War). Burnt Norton – mansion with interesting history
    (including arson) inspired poem by T.S. Eliot.

Dover's Hill is in the care of the NT. It was named after Robert Dover who founded his Cotswold Games in 1610. He was an army captain and his sports included shin kicking,

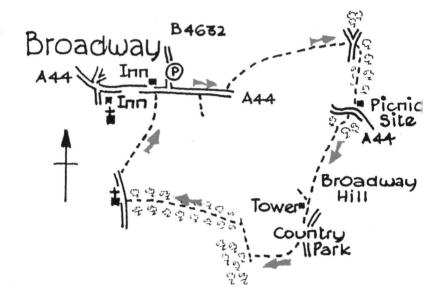

WALK 53

pitching the bar, single-stick fighting and walking on the hands. The pastimes continued for 200 years until they were stopped in 1841 because of 'rowdyism and brutality'. In recent years they have been revived in a gentler form.

Park at carpark in Chipping Campden. 154396. Opposite church take signed footpath around school (keep on left). Keep at edge of playing field then ahead by barns. Path is waymarked to lane. Turn left. At junction take drive opposite. Past farm follow blue waymark arrows. (Burnt Norton is to left.) Across parkland go over drive to left of farm. Continue to B4632. Turn left for 400 yards. Take footpath signed on left. Cross bridge. Walk at edge of field. Over stiles follow marked path then proceed at side of left-hand wood. There is high stile by gate. Take yellow-arrowed way along wide track to B4035. Cross to path opposite to pass trig. point to Dover's Hill. Retrace path for 400 yards. Turn right to lane. Turn left then right to Chipping Campden.

To shorten walk: Turn left at first road junction then right along B4035. Save two miles.

53. *Broadway Hill*

Distance of walk: 9.6km/6ml.
Distance from Birmingham: 54km/34ml.
Ordnance Survey maps: 150 and 1043.
Refreshments: Inns, tea-rooms, Broadway; restaurant and tea-room, Broadway country park.
Paths: Good, well-used tracks. Part of route is Cotswold Way.
Terrain: Typical Cotswold limestone countryside with sheep pastures and arable fields surrounded by stone walls.
Points of interest: Broadway village, said to be most picturesque in England (but spoiled somewhat by main-road traffic); prestigious Lygon Arms (once stage-coach inn); Broadway tower; Broadway country park (museum, nature trail, etc.); Fish Hill picnic site; St Eadburgha's Norman church.

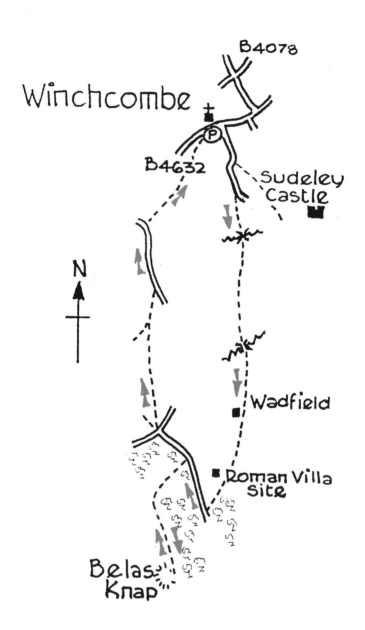

Winchcombe

B4078

B4632

Sudeley Castle

N

Wadfield

Roman Villa Site

Belas Knap

WALK 54

Broadway Hill is the second highest point in the Cotswolds at 1024ft. It is topped by a turreted tower built in 1797 (which adds 55ft to its height). The view from the summit is reputed to be the broadest in England, encompassing the Black Mountains and, according to tradition, 13 separate counties.

Park at carpark off B4632 in Broadway. 100377. From carpark proceed to A44. Turn left. Within half a mile take footpath on left. In pasture follow waymarks. A series of stiles shows way, climbing uphill to lane. Cross to stile and footpath. Clear path twists through beech-woods to Fish Hill picnic site (toposcope here). Go over main road to pick up Cotswold Way signs through woods to sheep pastures to Broadway Tower and country park. Keep ahead to pass to right of restaurant and go left to tarmac vehicle drive. Turn right. Bear right by new house to T-junction of tracks by wood. Turn right. Pick up clear track going left through elongated wood to road by St Eadburgha's church. Turn right. Within quarter of a mile path is signed on right to Broadway.

To shorten walk: Turn right by Broadway Tower. Follow Cotswold Way signs. Save two miles.

54.   Belas Knap

Distance of walk: 8km/5ml.
Distance from Birmingham: 80km/50ml.
Ordnance Survey maps: 144 and 1067.
Refreshments: Inns and cafés, Winchcombe.
Paths: Good, well-used paths; part of route along Cotswold Way.
Terrain: Upland tracks are over well-drained limestone; lower paths are over fields which can be damp.
Points of interest: Winchcombe was once capital of the kingdom of Mercia; St Peter's church dates from 1470 and has many weird gargoyles on the walls; old abbey site; Sudeley Castle is a Tudor castle and was the home of Catherine of Aragon (who lies buried in the castle chapel).

Belas Knap (from 'bel' a beacon and 'cnaepp' a hilltop) is the name of the long barrow which is situated at 900ft

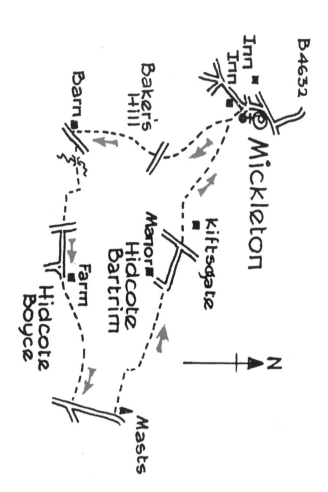

WALK 55

(274m) on a breezy ridge above Winchcombe. It was a Neolithic burial chamber and has been dated at between 4,000 and 3,000 BC.

Park at carpark in Winchcombe. 024282. Almost opposite church go along the lane signed to Sudeley Castle. Within third of a mile take path on right (now on Cotswold Way). Go over fields along clear track to gradually climb past fine Georgian house of Wadfield Farm (keep on right side). A little further Roman villa site (with well-preserved pavement) is in the trees right. Continue climb to lane. Turn right then take path left (signed Belas Knap) after a few hundred yards. Follow good path to barrow and retrace steps to lane. Turn left. At junction climb stile to sheep pasture. Two paths are signed; take right-hand one and descend steep hill along indicated direction. Join farm road and maintain heading to road. Turn left for quarter of a mile. Go over stone stile right and follow path back to Winchcombe.

The walk cannot be conveniently shortened.

55. Baker's Hill, Mickleton

Distance of walk: 9km/6ml.
Distance from Birmingham: 54km/34ml.
Ordance Survey maps: 151 and 1020.
Refreshments: Inns and hotel, Mickleton.
Paths: Well used and waymarked.
Terrain: Limestone uplands – arable and sheep farms.
Points of interest: Norman church with 600-year-old spire;
    Hidcote Manor; Manor Gardens (NT); Kiftsgate Gardens.

The paths follows a fine wood of mature beech trees which clothe Baker's Hill overlooking the flat Avon vale.

Park in cul-de-sac lane near Mickleton church. 162436. Just past church take right-hand path. Go at side of field and through elongated wood to pasture. Keep ahead then bear right alongside wood to lane. Cross to opposite path up bank to field. Follow edge to walk through wood of Baker's Hill to lane by barn. Go left then at once along signed path right. Drop down to bridge over brook. Follow edge of field (hedge

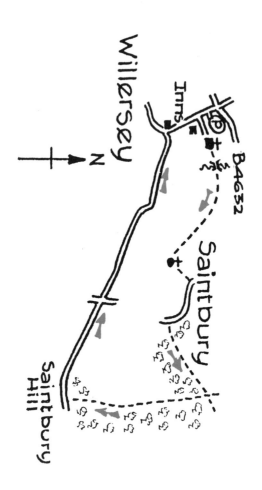

WALK 56

on left) around corners to hedge gap. Follow wide green track to road. Take opposite lane to Hidcote Boyce. Keep ahead through gate and climb track uphill. Through old quarries walk through gate in top-left corner to lane. Turn left (old drover's road). At mast take track left to Hidcote Gardens. Keep ahead along lane to junction. Cross to opposite path to Mickleton.

To shorten walk: Take path left through gate at Hidcote Boyce – saves one-and-a-half miles.

56. *Saintbury Hill*

Distance of walk: 5.5km/3.5ml.
Distance from Birmingham: 51km/32ml.
Ordnance Survey maps: 151 and 1020.
Refreshments: Inns, Willersey.
Paths: Good, well-waymarked route.
Terrain: Paths are through sheep pastures and woods.
Points of interest: Willersey, pretty Cotswold village with duck pond; Norman church with 600-year-old tower; part Saxon church at Saintbury.

Splendid view over Avon vale from Saintbury Hill; the spired church is not on top of the high hill, as is usual, but above orchards halfway up the escarpment.

Park in side roads off B4632. 117396 From the centre of Willersey walk along cul-de-sac lane to church. Enter churchyard and walk along left-hand border. Pass through kissing gate. In pasture walk to stile then another. The track divides. Keep ahead over further stiles then route bears right. There are more stiles (all waymarked) to Saintbury church. Walk along drive to lane. Turn right. Climb to signed bridleway on left. Walk through wood to drop down to junction of tracks. Turn right. When path divides take left fork. Climb uphill (brook on left side) to lane. Turn right and go straight over at crossroads. The steep banked lane drops down to Willersey.

To shorten walk: Take waymarked path behind Saintbury Church – saves one-and-a-half miles.

Dumbleton

P

Cricket
Ground

Farm

Dumbleton
Hill

Farm

To Alderton

N

WALK 57

57. Dumbleton Hill

Distance of walk: 5.5km/3.5ml.
Distance from Birmingham: 64km/40ml.
Ordnance Survey maps: 150 and 1043.
Refreshments: Should be carried.
Paths: Not all tracks on the route are well used but route-finding should not prove difficult.
Terrain: Mixed farmland, park and woods. Land drains well.
Points of interest: Old church with 700-year-old tower; fine Norman doorway.

This walk can be easily combined with the Alderton Hill walk to give an extended figure-of-eight route. Dumbleton Hill is crowned with fine woods.

Park in street at Dumbleton. 017360. Walk along Dairy Lane which becomes vehicle drive alongside cricket pitch. Climb stile in railing fence on right. Follow signed direction to go through tall trees to step-stile. Arrow shows heading over pasture to woods. Path runs alongside left-hand woods which cover Dumbleton Hill to farm. Turn left, picking up Wychavon Way signs. Climb to Oxhill Wood. Go right then

Walk 58   The path to Alderton Hill

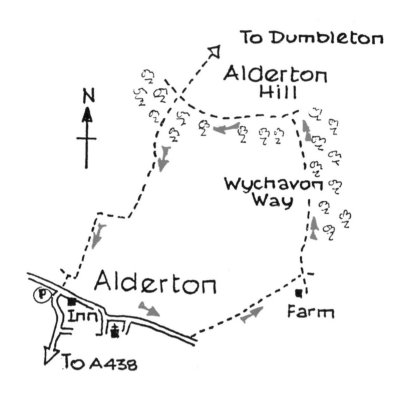

To Dumbleton

Alderton
Hill

Wychavon
Way

N

Alderton

Inn

P

To A438

Farm

WALK 58

left, following clear track through larches and across a ride and along top of plantation. Fork left to reach farm cart-track. Turn left along this track. Pass farm and descend to lane to Dumbleton.

58. *Alderton Hill*

Distance of walk: 4.5km/3ml.
Distance from Birmingham: 64km/40ml.
Ordnance Survey maps: 150 and 1043.
Refreshments: Inn, Alderton.
Paths: Mostly good, well-used tracks; part of walk is along the waymarked Wychavon Way.
Terrain: Mixed farmland and woods.
Points of interest: Ancient church with Saxon and Norman work; tower is fifteenth century.

Alderton Hill is an outlier of the Cotswolds. Alderton is an old settlement as the name – farmstead of the (Saxon) Aldhere – indicates.

Park in a street in Alderton. 999333. From inn walk along Dibden Lane towards church. Within half a mile is double footpath sign on left. Take left-hand way, aiming over pasture towards left of farm. Join waymarked route of Wychavon Way and turn left. Follow arrows, gradually climbing uphill through fields and woods. At crossing on farm track leave Wychavon Way to turn left. The farm track twists downhill to emerge in Alderton conveniently near inn.

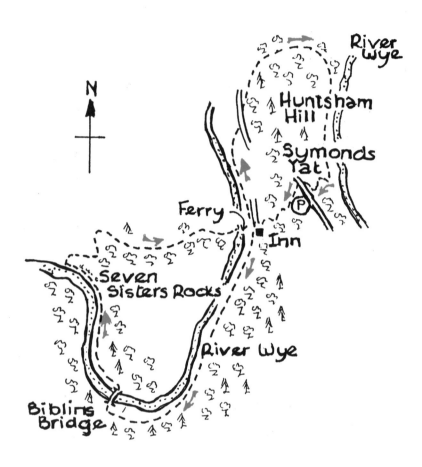

N

River Wye

Huntsham Hill

Symonds Yat

P

Ferry

Inn

Seven Sisters Rocks

River Wye

Biblins Bridge

WALK 59

59. *Symonds Yat and Seven Sisters Rocks*

Distance of walk: 9km/6ml.
Distance from Birmingham: 115km/72ml.
Ordnance Survey maps: 162 and 1087. Outdoor Leisure map
   no. 14 (Wye Valley).
Refreshments: Inn and kiosk, Symonds Yat.
Paths: Good, well-used tracks. Part of route is Wye Valley
   Path.
Terrain: Sandy and rocky through woods. Can be muddy by
   river.
Points of interest: Yat Rock – spectacular vantage point;
   King Arthur's Cave (did Merlin bury Arthur's treasure
   here?); Biblins suspension bridge.

Route follows wooded slopes above River Wye. Beside the
river (a favourite spot for canoeists) a track goes along
picturesque former railway line. A favourite walk for
autumn.

Park in carpark at Symonds Yat Rock. 564158. Walk few
steps along lane northwards under footbridge. Take path on
left which drops steeply down through trees to river. Turn left
past inn to pick up rail route (Wye Valley Walk signs) to
Biblins suspension bridge to cross river. Turn left. Within a
mile take path climbing right – track through beech trees to
Seven Sisters Rocks and King Arthur's Cave. Follow clear
path to descend to riverside path. Turn left to village and
ferry to cross river. Turn left along lane then follow riverside
track past caravan site (again on Wye Valley Walk path).
Follow waymark arrows to cross lane. Path skirts around
Huntsham Hill then climbs steeply through trees to Symonds
Yat Rock.

To shorten walk: Retrace steps after ferry – saves one mile.

Masts

Foxcote

Ebrington Hill

Shelter

House

Barns

Hut

House

N

P

Inn

Ebrington

WALK 60

60. Ebrington Hill

Distance of walk: 9km/6ml.
Distance from Birmingham: 60km/37ml.
Ordnance Survey maps: 151 and 1020/1021.
Refreshments: Inn, Ebrington.
Paths: Some not defined on the ground and unofficially
    diverted at times.
Terrain: Limestone hills which drain well.
Points of interest: Ebrington church has fine Norman
    doorway with carvings; Foxcote is early eighteenth-
    century mansion.

The walk climbs above the village and is one of the first hills
of the Cotswolds. There are fine views in all directions.

Park in street at Ebrington village. 185400. From village
green by inn walk along lane signed to Mickleton. Keep
ahead at junction. Climb stone stile on right between houses.
Take left-hand path. Follow waymarked route at side of
playing field then keep ahead over stiles and bridges.
Undefined path climbs steadily then goes by house (path may
be diverted) to farm cart-track. Keep on same heading over
large arable field towards elongated wood. Follow edge
(trees on right) to lane. Turn right for 400 yards. Take wide
farm 'road' on right. Walk by tall masts. Follow track to lane.
Just past woods (on left) take cart-track on right. Go by
woods to pasture. Walk to far left corner by shelter. Through
gate follow waymarks to barns. At far side take waymarked
path to right. Go left then cross water. Regain heading for few
steps (brook now on left). Turn 90 degrees right. Climb ridge.
Turn left along tractor way to road. Turn right to Ebrington.

To shorten walk: Turn right at elongated wood then right
along farm 'road' (saves one-and-a-half miles).

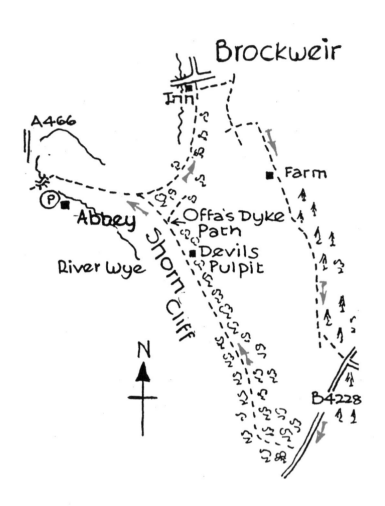

Brockweir

A466

Inn

Farm

P
Abbey

Offa's Dyke
Path

Devils
Pulpit

River Wye

Shorn Cliff

N

B4228

WALK 61

61. Shorn Cliff and Devil's Pulpit

Distance of walk: 11km/7ml.
Distance from Birmingham: 128km/80ml.
Ordnance Survey maps: 162 and 1111. Outdoor Leisure map
no. 14 (Wye Valley).
Refreshments: Inn, Brockweir.
Paths: Good, well-used tracks. Parts of Offa's Dyke Path
used.
Terrain: Route is mainly along rugged tracks through woods.
Most of route drains well.
Points of interest: Ruins of Cistercian Tintern Abbey; Offa's
Dyke; Devil's Pulpit (rocky outcrop where Devil is said to
have preached to monks in Abbey).

The route follows the line of Offa's Dyke for three miles at
the edge of the plateau above Shorn Cliff. The path is mainly
through woods but there are plenty of gaps to enjoy the river
view.

Park at carpark of Tintern Abbey. 530003. Cross river over
old rail bridge. Keep along route of old railway to hamlet of
Brockweir. Just before village take track right (signed as
alternative Offa's Dyke Path route). Join main Dyke Path.
Turn right. Through woods emerge by metal posts to bold
crossing track. Turn left over stile. Continue to further
corner-stile. Turn 90 degrees right alongside right-hand
fence to farm. Keep to left of barns to walk along hedged
green road to rough lane. Just past Offa's Dyke sign go
through gateway on left. Follow edge of woods (marked to
Tidenham) to B4228. Turn right for three-quarters of a mile.
Climb stile on right to walk through Fidenham section of
Dyke. Cross two vehicle-tracks passing the rocks of Devil's
pulpit. Follow signs for Tintern. Join outward route over
river to carpark.

This walk cannot easily be shortened.

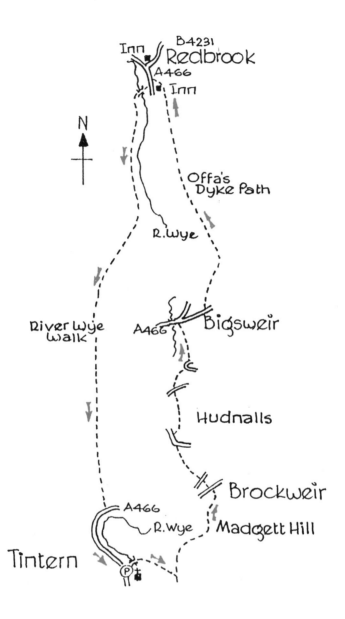

WALK 62

62. The Hudnalls and Madgett Hill

Distance of walk: 25.5km/16ml.
Distance from Birmingham: 128km/80ml.
Ordnance Survey maps: 162 and 1111. Outdoor Leisure map
   no. 14 (Wye Valley).
Refreshments: Inns, Redbrook, Brockweir.
Paths: Good, well-used tracks. Route uses Wye Valley Path
   and pastoral lands.
Points of interest: Well-preserved sections of Offa's Dyke;
   ruins of Tintern Abbey.

The walk is along the upland slopes high above the River
Wye with magnificent continuous views. It returns to Tintern
on a well-waymarked lowland route. The woods are
especially beautiful in autumn.

Park in carpark at Tintern Abbey. 530003. Cross river by
bridge which once carried rail route. Follow Offa's Dyke
Path signs to walk through woodlands of Caswell Wood and
Lippets Grove and over Madgett Hill. When official path
route divides keep to right-hand upland way. Cross valley

Walk 63   The ruins of Hailes Abbey

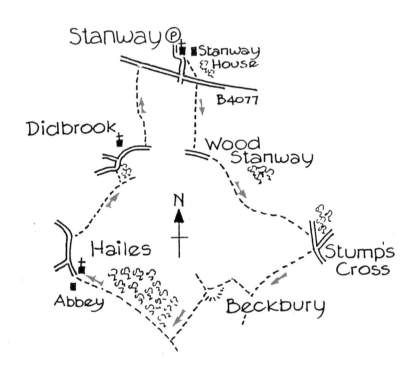

WALK 63

near Brockweir then follow waymarks along paths and lanes bordering St Briavels Common and over Hudnalls Walk through dense woods then descend to Wye and A466 at Bigsweir. Turn right along lane (sign St Briavels). After half a mile turn left along vehicle-track then follow path through woods, field and scrubland. Drop down to main road at Redland. Cross road and go over River Wye. Join River Wye Path. Route back to Tintern is waymarked.

To shorten walk: Cross river at Bigsweir – saves eight miles.

63. Beckbury Hill-Fort

Distance of walk: 9km/6ml.
Distance from Birmingham: 64km/40ml.
Ordnance Survey maps: 150 and 1043.
Refreshments: Should be carried.
Paths: Good. Part of route along Cotswold Way.
Terrain: Limestone uplands; sheeplands and lanes.
Points of interest: Ditches and ramparts of Beckbury Fort; ruins of Hailes Abbey (Cistercian); twelfth-century Hailes church (wall paintings); Stanway House (seventeenth century); stump of medieval cross at Stumps Cross.

The feature of this walk is the hill-fort on a lofty strategic site on the scarp edge of the Cotswolds.

Park in road at Stanway. 061323. Near church follow path (Cotswold Way) to B4077. Cross to opposite path to hamlet of Wood Stanway. Turn left and follow Cotswold Way signs past farmsteads to Stumps Cross. Turn right on B4077 then right along cart-track (signed Farmcote). Follow CW waymarks to Beckbury Hill-Fort. Drop down to farm 'road'. Turn right to Hailes and lane. Quarter of a mile past Abbey (on bend) take path down cart-track right. At junction of paths at three-quarters of a mile turn left through meadow to lane at Didbrook. Go right. Just before wood take signed path left to B4077. Stanway is right.

To shorten walk: Take path from Wood Stanway that borders right-hand woodlands to Beckbury. Saves one-and-a-half miles.

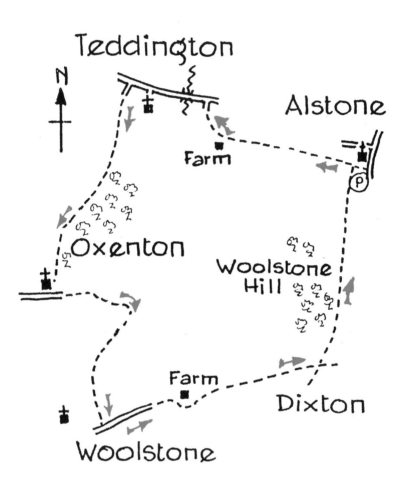

Teddington

Alstone

N

Farm

Oxenton

Woolstone
Hill

Farm

Dixton

Woolstone

WALK 64

64. Woolstone Hill

Distance of walk: 9km/6ml.
Distance from Birmingham: 64km/40ml.
Ordnance Survey maps: 150 and 1043.
Refreshments: Should be carried.
Paths: Most are good and waymarked.
Terrain: Limestone uplands which drain well.
Points of interest: Old churches (Norman work) in each
    village; scratch dials on walls.

Walk is around rim of Woolstone Hill – an outlier of the
Cotswolds.

Park in road at Alstone near church. 983325. Near church
path is signed up vehicle-track. Path divides. Keep ahead
through gate. Series of stiles shows route through sheep
pasture and along cart-track to lane. Turn right then left at T-
junction to Teddington. Pass church and turn left down lane.
Beyond farm buildings look for waymarked stile. Follow
further waymarks to wood then path leads to Oxenton
church. Walk through churchyard to lane. Turn left to farm
track (marked as footpath) around hillside towards wood.

Follow path arrows – path is beside wood to open moor;
walk around Crane Hill then descend to farm and lane at
Woolstone. Turn left to barns then continue to bold track
coming from farmstead. Climb hill to old barn. Turn right to
keep by wire fence. Go over ditch to tractor way, now aiming
towards Dixton Hill. Follow waymarks to junction of paths.
Take path signed left, now climbing towards Woolstone Hill.
Keep at right-hand border of field. Waymarks lead to side of
wood. When border veers left keep ahead on old direction.
Climb stile to right of large barn. Cross plank bridge. Further
stiles mark route to Alstone.

This walk cannot be shortened.

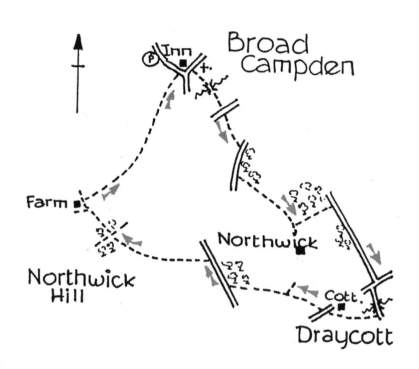

WALK 65

65. Northwick Hill

Distance of walk: 6.5km/4ml.
Distance from Birmingham: 59km/37ml.
Ordnance Survey maps: 151 and 1043.
Refreshments: Inn, Broad Campden.
Paths: Good, clear tracks – part of route is Heart of England Way.
Terrain: Mixed landscape – woods, arable and meadowland on mainly limestone soils.
Points of interest: Northwick House – seventeenth-century mansion; Polish monument; St Michael's church, Broad Campden.

The hills are gentle rises looking out over typical Cotswold countryside. There are pretty villages with thatched houses.

Park in quiet roads at village of Broad Campden. 157377. By St Michael's Church go along signed path. Fenced way goes over brook to lane, which cross. Go up steps to meadow. Take waymarked direction over rough land to stile to lane. Turn right. Stay on lane for quarter of a mile. Take farm drive on left. Keep on concrete drive alongside left-hand wood. Climb stile by gate. Turn 90 degrees left along estate road past industrial units and Polish memorial (needs rescuing) to stile to lane. Turn right. Go past entrance to Northwick House. At T-junction turn right then at once take lane left. Cross brook. Take signed path right. Follow waymarked route to reach house drive to lane. Cross to tarmac way opposite. After 300 yards tarmac way twists sharp right. Climb stile on left. Walk over field to stile to woods. Follow clear track to large pasture. Walk near right-hand border to road. Turn right. Within half a mile take signed bridleway left. Follow blue waymark arrows to walk through hunting gate then alongside left-hand hedge. At junction of ways keep ahead to elongated woods. Maintain heading to farm. Path is signed through gate to right of house. Follow Heart of England Way waymarks back to Broad Campden.

To shorten walk: Keep along lane at first farm drive. Saves two miles.

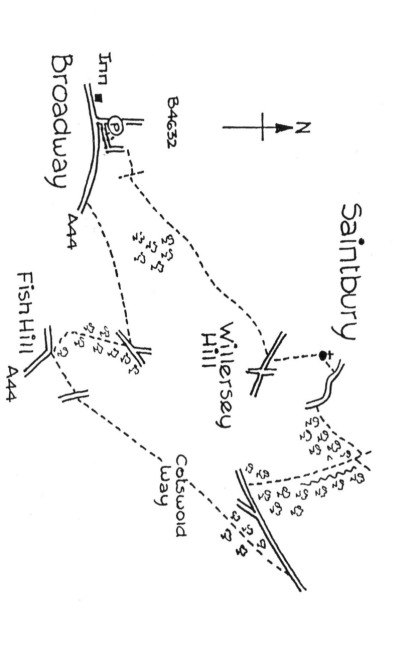

WALK 66

66. Willersey Hill

Distance of walk: 13km/8ml.
Distance from Birmingham: 72km/45ml.
Ordnance Survey maps: 150 and 1043.
Refreshments: Inns, and cafés, Broadway.
Paths: Good but not always marked on ground. Part of route
   is Cotswold Way,
Terrain: Limestone soils – route mixed woods, arable and
   pastoral farmland.
Points of interest: Broadway is pretty village with many
   antique shops and art galleries in which to window gaze;
   picnic site with toposcope on Fish Hill.

Willersey Hill overlooks the valley of the River Avon and
Vale of Evesham; there is a golf course on the hill with
spectacular views.

Park in carpark on B4632 off Broadway High Street.
100377. Go along path at back of park to estate road. Turn
left and left again at end of road. Pick up signed path around
gardens. Cross road along fenced way. Follow arrowed path
over farm road. Climb hill along waymarked route. Cross
vehicle way and keep at side of golf course. Cross lane.
Climb stone stile. Walk to Saintbury church. Walk along
drive to lane. Turn right for quarter of a mile. Turn left along
bridleway. Go through wood to meeting of paths. Turn right.
Walk through woods and pastures (brook on left) to lane.
Turn left and left again at junction. Within third of a mile take
path (Cotswold Way) on right. Follow signed way to Fish
Hill picnic site (crossing lane on way). Turn right. Follow
path through woods to lane. Cross to opposite path over stile.
Walk through sheep pasture to A44. Broadway is to right.

To shorten walk: Turn right on lane after golf course. Turn
right at crossroads and first right at next junction. Saves four
miles.

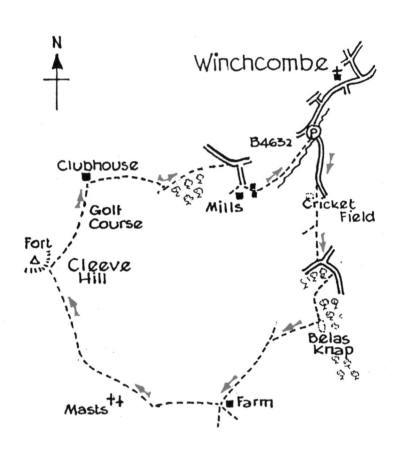

WALK 67

67.   Cleeve Hill

Distance of walk: 13km/8ml.
Distance from Birmingham: 80km/50ml.
Ordnance Survey maps: 163 and 1066/1067.
Refreshments: Café (Cleeve Hill golf club).
Paths: Well-used tracks – some difficulty with multiplicity of
    tracks on Cleeve Common. Part of route along Cotswold
    Way.
Terrain: Limestone Cotswold uplands – rocky in places.
    Route through sheep pasture, arable fields and over golf
    course.
Points of interest: Belas Knap Barrow, Cleeve Common,
    Paper mill on old site. Cleeve hill-fort.

Cleeve Hill is the highest point of the Cotswolds at over
1,000ft. The Ancient Britons knew where to site their camp
for the best viewpoint.
    Park in lay-by quarter of a mile along B4632 west of
Winchcombe. 018278. Take lane (Corndean Lane) signed to
Brockhampton. After third of a mile take path signed right
along drive of Corndean Hall. Past cricket pitch drive twists
sharp right. Keep old direction over stile. Climb through
sheep pastures to stile to lane. Keep ahead few steps to path
right signed to Belas Knap. Follow path to barrow. Pick up
Cotswold Way waymarks and follow route at edge of field.
Continue to follow arrowed way past farm and climb to
Cleeve Common. Keep to right of masts and along path over
golf course to earthwork called The Ring. Swing right to golf
clubhouse (in hollow but ask a golfer if in doubt of direction).
Take signed path right along wide cart-track beside left-hand
wall. Keep ahead out of golf course and beside wood to
B4632. Turn right. Within 200 yards take lane right to paper
mill. Keep left when lane divides. By warehouse waymark
arrow on pillar. Take way left along vehicle way. Walk past
bungalows. When way turns sharp left keep ahead over stile.
Follow path to lay-by.
    Walk cannot easily be shortened.

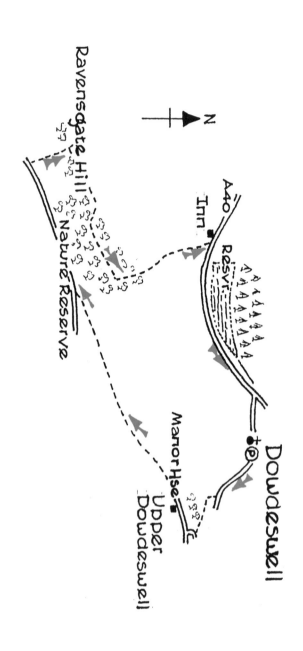

WALK 68

68. Ravensgate Hill

Distance of walk: 8km/5ml.
Distance from Birmingham: 80km/50ml.
Ordnance Survey maps: 163 and 1089/1090.
Refreshments: Inn, Dowdeswell.
Paths: Not all marked on ground but clear. Part of route along Cotswold Way.
Terrain: Route over pasture and through woods. Tracks can be muddy.
Points of interest: Woodland Nature Reserve; Dowdeswell church (with central spire) has 300-year-old sundial and Tudor porch; reservoir (supplies Cheltenham).

Ravensgate Hill is a steep little upland on the Cotswold Way. There are fine woods here – especially attractive in spring.

There is limited parking near church. 001199. Climb hill along lane alongside right-hand wall. Within third of a mile go right. Path is signed through tall metal kissing gate. Take direction indicated, aiming to left of row of tall poplars. Climb field to stile to vehicle drive. Turn right, passing cottage to hamlet of Upper Dowdeswell. Turn right on lane. Past manor house lane becomes a wide bridleway. Keep ahead to A436. Turn right. Pass Woodland Trust Nature Reserve. (Visitors welcome.) Within three-quarters of a mile take path (Cotswold Way) right. Cross arable field. Follow waymarked (CW) route to turn right to drop down steep slope of Ravensgate Hill. The path goes through Lineover ('lime-tree hill') Wood then descends to cross old rail route. On A40 turn right. Main road but pleasant footpath alongside reservoir. At end turn right along lane to Dowdeswell.

Walk cannot be shortened.

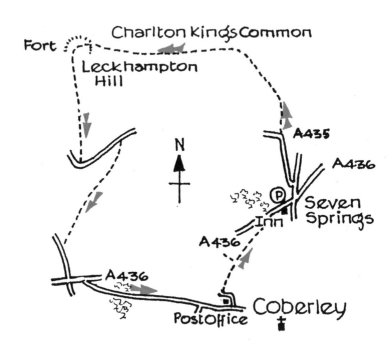

WALK 69

69. Leckhampton Hill

Distance of walk: 8km/5ml.
Distance from Birmingham: 80km/50ml.
Ordnance Survey maps: 163 and 1089.
Refreshments: Inn, Seven Springs.
Paths: Good, well-used paths; part of route is Cotswold Way.
Terrain: Route is through arable farmland and old quarry area.
Points of interest: Rock shapes on Leckhampton Hill; old hill-fort; Dick Whittington lived at Coberley; Coberley church sundial was built in 1693; nineteenth-century parcel house at Seven Springs.

The walk starts at Seven Springs – one of the sources of River Thames. Leckhampton Hill is a magnificent viewpoint on a Cotswold spur. On return route passes through Coberley – often wins 'best-kept village' competition.

Park in large lay-by opposite inn along A436 from Seven Springs junction. 967170. Turn left to junction. (Note round parcel house.) Turn left along A435. Within few steps take unsigned lane left. Within half a mile lane twists sharp left. Keep ahead along well-used footpath (Cotswold Way). Follow waymarked path through Charlton Kings Common to Leckhampton Hill. Keep following waymark arrows to drop to lane. Turn left. Within 400 yards take path along wide stony way to right. On lane turn left to main road. Turn left for 200 yards. Turn right along lane signed to Coberley. Gated road passes farms and leads to Coberley. By post office (in same family for over 100 years) turn left. Lane passes old cross. By terraced houses take wide cart-track ahead. (Path is signed Seven Springs.) Way climbs steadily uphill and maintains direction then goes around arable field to A436. Carpark is to right.

To shorten walk: Stay on lane after descending from Leckhampton Hill. Saves one mile.

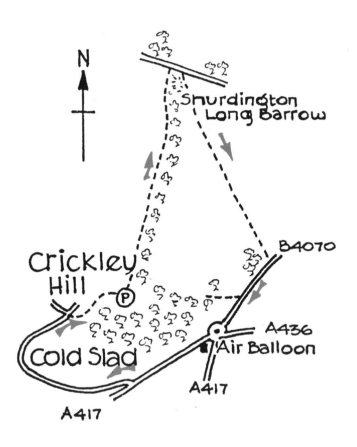

N

Shurdington
Long Barrow

B4070

Crickley
Hill

P

A436

Cold Slad

Air Balloon

A417

A417

WALK 70

70. Crickley Hill

Distance of walk: 6.5km/4ml.
Distance from Birmingham: 80km/50ml.
Ordnance Survey maps: 163 and 1089.
Refreshments: Inn, Air Balloon junction.
Paths: Good, well-used tracks. Part of route is Cotswold Way.
Terrain: Walk is through pastures and woods. Extensive quarry workings at Crickley Hill.
Points of interest: Crickley hill-fort; Shurdington Long Barrow (on private land).

The walk starts from Crickley Hill country park where there is much natural history and archaeological activity during the year.

Park in top carpark. 930164. From the corner of the carpark climb steps to stile to pasture. Follow waymarked Cotswold Way path at edge of fields then through the beeches of Short Wood. Follow path to steps down to lane. Turn right for 100 yards. Take bridleway (blue arrow) on right. Shurdington Long Barrow is to right. Follow bridleway to B4090. Turn right to road junction. Turn right along main road A417. Within half a mile take lane right signed Cold Slad. Go through hamlet. At junction of ways (lane marked 'unfit for motors') take bridleway (blue arrow) on right. Track climbs through rough land to lower carpark of Crickley Hill. Walk up steps to top carpark.

To shorten walk: Take car entrance to Crickley Hill country park from B4070. Saves one mile.

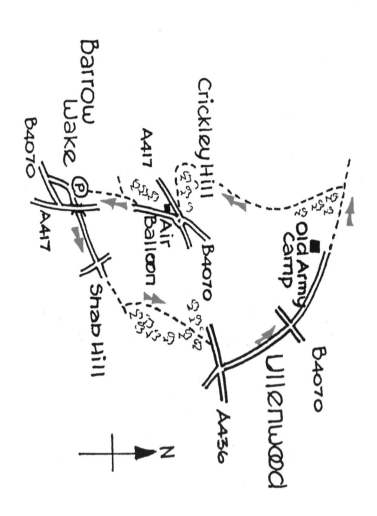

WALK 71

71. *Barrow Wake*

Distance of walk: 9km/6ml.
Distance from Birmingham: 80km/50ml.
Ordnance Survey maps: 163 and 1089.
Refreshments: Inn, Air Balloon junction.
Paths: Most are good but not all are marked on the ground; part of route along Cotswold Way.
Terrain: Walk is through woods and farmland.
Points of interest: Barrow Wake is important archaeological site – plenty of display information by carpark; rocky outcrop called Devil's Table.

The walk starts on the hilltop with wide views over the Severn valley. The county council has made the place popular by providing carparks and easy access.

Park in carpark at Barrow Wake. 930152. Take lane which goes under main road (signed to Shab Hill). At crossroads after half a mile keep ahead. Within another half a mile take footpath over stile by wood left. In field take signed direction gradually leaving right-hand wood. Enter woods and, keeping same heading, continue to A436. Turn right for third of a mile. Take lane on left signed to Ullenwood. At B4090 cross to Greenway Lane. Lane goes past old army camp. The way enters woods. At end climb steps left. The path goes over stile. Follow Cotswold Way and follow waymarks to Crickley Hill. Keep along Cotswold Way, passing Devil's Table.

Drop down hill then walk through meadowland to hunting gate on to Air Balloon junction. Cross by inn and walk along A417. Within 400 yards and by phone box take unsigned path right along tarmac way below main road. Keep ahead when Cotswold Way is signed to right to return to carpark at Barrow Wake.

The walk cannot easily be shortened.

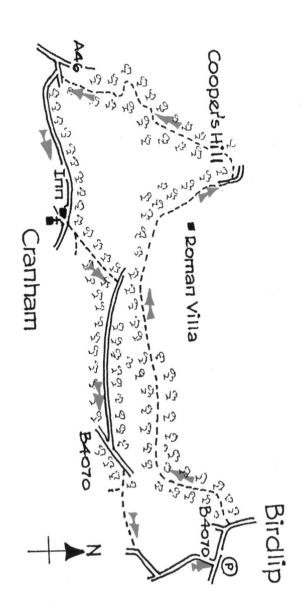

WALK 72

72. *Cooper's Hill*

Distance of walk: 14km/9ml.
Distance from Birmingham: 83km/52ml.
Ordnance Survey maps: 162/163 and 1089.
Refreshments: Inns, Birdlip and Cranham.
Paths: Most paths are well used; part of route is Cotswold Way.
Terrain: Much of outward route is through deciduous woodlands; some quiet lanes are used for the return.
Points of interest: Cooper's Hill is famous cheese-rolling slope – country sport which takes place at Spring Bank Holiday. Contestants chase seven-lb cheese down 1:1 slope – the winner keeps it; Witcombe Roman villa.

Park along quiet streets of Birdlip – now by-passed and quiet. 926144. Take B4070 out of village towards Stroud. At once B4070 twists sharp left. Keep ahead along road signed to the Witcombes which drops sharply downhill. Within 200 yards take signed (Cotswold Way) path through woods to left. Follow waymarked path to Cooper's Hill (diverting to Witcombe Roman villa if interested). Path drops through Brockworth Wood (interesting notices on natural features) to road. Turn left then take lane on right signed to Cranham. Shop has closed but there is still a pub. Just beyond pub and opposite phone box turn left along signed path. Past a house (Treetops) track divides. Take left-hand way and keep on straight heading to road. Turn right. Bear left at junction. Within 300 yards take signed bridleway on right. Through trees keep ahead to green road. Follow this to lane. Keep ahead to T-junction. Turn left to Birdlip.

This walk cannot conveniently be shortened.

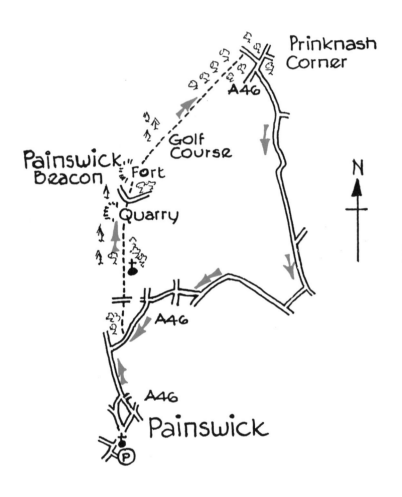

WALK 73

73. Painswick Beacon

Distance of walk: 9km/6ml.
Distance from Birmingham: 83km/52ml.
Ordnance Survey maps: 162 and 1089.
Refreshments: Inns, Painswick.
Paths: All paths used are waymarked; Cotswold Way;
    numerous other tracks on Painswick Hill.
Terrain: Wooded upland heaths partly covered by golf
    course.
Points of interest: Painswick village called 'the jewel of the
    Cotswolds' (wealth was based on old wool trade); 174ft-
    high spire; famous yew trees in churchyard (99 of them –
    or is it 100?); hill-fort on Beacon.

The upland was used as a signal station. Beacons were lit to
convey messages. Now it is a good viewpoint.
    Park in carpark south of church. 866096. Walk to main
A46 road. Turn right to keep church on right. Continue
through village. By one-way street system (controlled by
lights) turn left along Gloucester Street to B4073. Turn left
for 300 yards. Turn right along Golf Course Road. After few
hundred yards look for Cotswold Way sign along path left.
Follow waymarked route to cross lane and alongside
churchyard. Pass Cotsbrain Quarry and follow to lane. Cross
and continue to follow Cotswold Way waymarks. Path is
over golf course with Painswick Beacon (and hill-fort) away
to left. Follow route through Buckholt Wood (National
Nature Reserve) to lane. Turn right to A46. Turn right for few
steps. Turn left along lane. Follow narrow lanes going right
at junctions to A46. Cross to lane. At crossroads turn left.
Follow outward route to Painswick.
    To shorten walk: On lane after Cotsbrain Quarry turn left
along signed bridleway. Saves three miles.

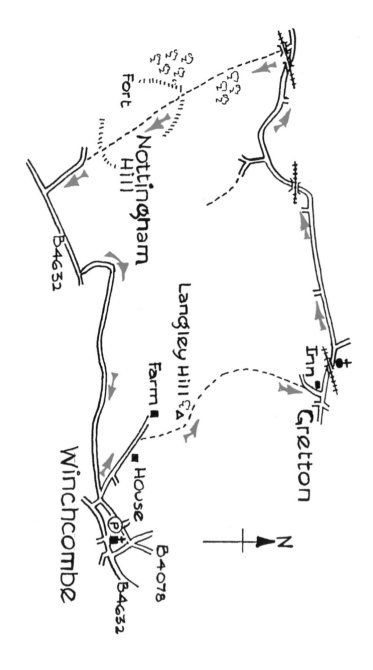

WALK 74

74. *Nottingham Hill*

Distance of walk: 14km/9ml.
Distance from Birmingham: 80km/50ml.
Ordnance Survey maps: 150/163 and 1066/1067.
Refreshments: Inns and cafés, Winchcombe; inn, Gretton.
Paths: Good, well-used tracks; part of route is along Wychavon Way.
Terrain: Nottingham Hill is outlier of limestone Cotswolds; route is through woods and rough pasture.
Points of interest: Ancient hill-fort on Nottingham Hill covering about 180 acres; Winchcombe (once a capital of region of Mercia); St Peter's church dated 1470 and old abbey site; Gretton thirteenth-century chapel tower.

Nottingham Hill rises some 600ft above the valley; with steep slopes it made an ideal site for a hill-fort.

Use carpark in Winchcombe. 023284. Turn left along Back Lane. Turn right (Harvey's Villas) then right again (Harvey's Lane). The rough lane goes over cattle-grid. Seventy-five yards beyond take signed path over stile right. Follow direction indicated over rough pasture. Follow Wychavon Way signs over stiles and through fields below hill-fort on Langley Hill. Drop down to walk along hedged way to Duglinch Lane at Gretton. At junction by Bugatti Inn turn left. (The Bugatti was famous type of Italian car used on Prescott Hill climbs.) Follow lanes (signed Gotherington). After two miles of lane walking take rough lane left. Go under railway bridge and vehicle-way becomes rough bridleway climbing steeply. The bridleway becomes farm cart-track across plateau top of Nottingham Hill. Keep ahead to lane. Maintain heading. Road borders narrow common where gypsies often camp. At B4632 turn left for two-thirds of a mile. Take unsigned lane left. This leads to Winchcombe.

To shorten walk: Turn left along lane (quarter of a mile past second rail bridge). When lane divides bear left. Lane becomes bridleway. Saves two miles.

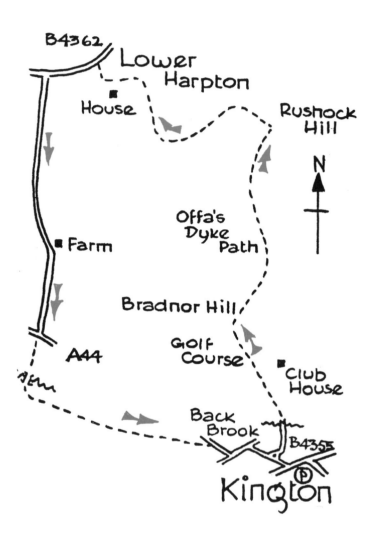

WALK 75

HEREFORDSHIRE

75. *Rushock Hill, Offa's Dyke*

Distance of walk: 11km/7ml.
Distance from Birmingham: 96km/60ml.
Ordance Survey maps: 148 and 993.
Refreshments: Inns, Kington.
Paths: Good tracks; part of route along Offa's Dyke Path.
Terrain: Mixed rough sheep uplands and woods.
Points of interest: Offa's Dyke; Norman church, Kington.

The hill section contains a fine section of the border marked by Offa (King of Mercia) with a bank and ditch about AD 700. An earlier hill (Bradnor Hill) carries one of the highest golf courses in England.

   Park at carpark in Kington. 294568. Walk along A44 towards church. Beyond war memorial turn right and drop down hill to Back Brook. Go left in front of cottages to bridge over river. Follow Offa's Dyke 'acorn' signs to reach the heathlands of National Trust. Signed path is over golf course then past farms and woods. Follow good section of the Dyke, now climbing Rushock Hill then swinging left alongside plantations. Path is around the 1,220ft Herrock Hill (keep on left). Follow path signs to lane and B4632. Turn left. Within 400 yards turn left along lane by cottage. Quiet way leads to A44. Cross road to gate opposite and keep ahead over brook. At farm track turn left and follow route to Kington.

   This walk cannot be conveniently shortened.

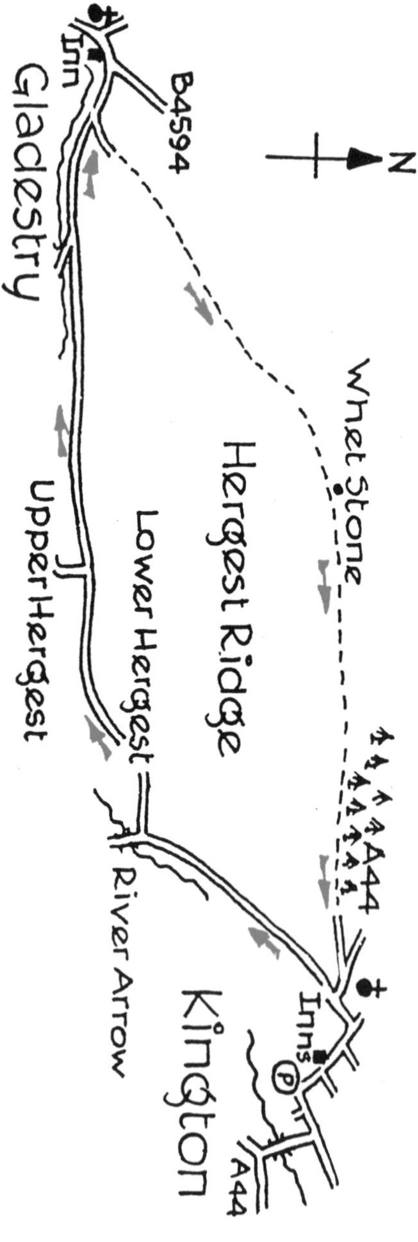

B4594

Glacestry

Inn

N

Whet Stone

Hergest Ridge

Upper Hergest

Lower Hergest

River Arrow

A44

Kington

Inns

P

A44

WALK 76

76. *Hergest Ridge*

Distance of walk: 16km/10ml.
Distance from Birmingham: 136km/85ml.
Ordnance Survey maps: 148 and 993.
Refreshments: Inns, Kington and Gladestry.
Paths: Route is along Offa's Dyke Path; although well waymarked (acorn symbol) the paths are a little indistinct in places.
Terrain: Hergest Ridge is open grazing land with a mixture of grass, bracken and gorse.
Points of interest: Norman church at Kington; Gladestry Court on site of manor; Whet stone – huge, isolated boulder on ridgetop; old racecourse site; Victorian buildings in Kington.

Hergest Ridge is three miles long and makes good walking on springy turf. There are magnificent views from the 1,400ft height over Radnor Forest.

Park in carpark in Kington. 297567. Walk along Church Road. Near church main road twists sharp right. Keep ahead on old direction. Lane follows River Arrow through Lower and Upper Hergest then along valley of Gladestry Brook to Gladestry – rather scattered village. Just before village Offa's Dyke Path is signed down cul-de-sac lane on right. This leads to cart-track gradually climbing up Hergest Ridge to plateau summit. Follow waymarked route (acorn signs on posts) through gorse and bracken, passing Whet Stone and old racecourse. Path drops over Haywood Common and past woods. Track becomes lane to emerge on A44 by St Mary's Church.

Walk cannot easily be shortened.

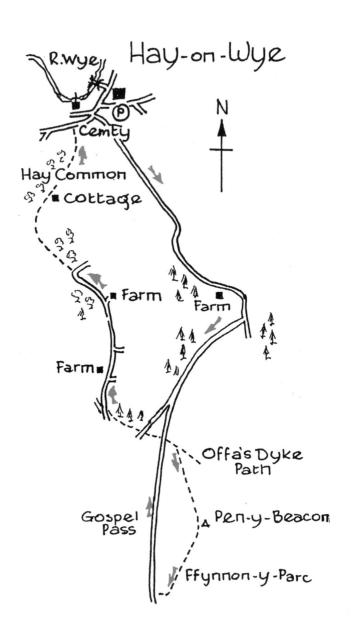

Hay-on-Wye

R.Wye

N

Cemty

Hay Common

Cottage

Farm

Farm

Farm

Offa's Dyke
Path

Gospel
Pass

Pen-y-Beacon

Ffynnon-y-Parc

WALK 77

77. *Pen-y-Beacon, Black Mountains*

Distance of walk: 16km/10ml.
Distance from Birmingham: 144km/90ml.
Ordnance Survey maps: 161 and 1016/1039.
Refreshments: Inns and cafés, Hay-on-Wye.
Paths: Well-used tracks – sometimes undefined on mountain.
   Return route is waymarked Offa's Dyke Path.
Terrain: A mixture of rocky moorland and mountain, narrow
   lanes through deciduous woods and common land.
Points of interest: Hay Castle built in 1150s; St Mary's
   church at Hay built 1120; Hay is centre for second-hand
   book shops; Offa's Dyke Path.

Offa's Dyke Path nudges Pen-y-Fan (or Hay Beacon to
Hereford folk) which is the most northern peak of Black
Mountains. At 2,219ft it is highest point of the long-distance
path. There are glorious views over wooded foothills of the
Wye valley.
   Park in carpark opposite castle. 226421. Turn left then left
again along Church Street. Almost opposite alms-houses
turn left along lane signed to Capel-y-ffin. When lane divides
take right fork then right again at next meeting of lanes. After
further mile there is another junction. Just beyond take path
left (Offa's Dyke Path). The path divides. Take track right
(alternative Dyke Path route) to trig plinth on summit of Pen-
y-Beacon. Follow ridge south-west then where convenient
swing right to descend to unenclosed road called Gospel
Pass. Turn right. Beyond carpark area take signed Offa's
Dyke Path over bracken area left. Cross road and keep old
heading (path waymarked) to rejoin road. Turn right for one-
and-a-half miles. On sharp bend take waymarked path on left
to walk by woods and over common. Follow signs to B4350.
Hay-on-Wye is to the right.
   The walk cannot conveniently be shortened.

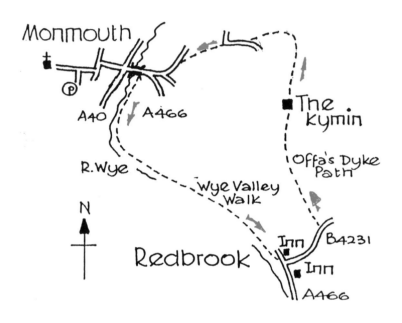

WALK 78

GWENT

78. *The Kymin*

Distance of walk: 9km/6ml.

Distance from Birmingham: 120km/75ml.

Ordnance Survey maps: 162 and 1087. Outdoor Leisure map
no. 14 (Wye Valley).

Refreshments: Inns and cafés, Monmouth; inns, Redbrook.

Paths: Good tracks; part of route along waymarked Wye
Valley Walk and Offa's Dyke Path.

Terrain: Route starts alongside River Wye then climbs
steeply through woods and meadows to The Kymin.

Points of interest: The Kymin is an 800ft hill overlooking the
River Wye. It is on National Trust land and has a
monument (built 1800) to honour the Royal Navy;
Monnow Gate (1272) is unique fortified gateway.

Park at carpark in centre of Monmouth. 508128. Walk along
St Mary's and Wyebridge streets to cross A40. Pass site of
Wye Gate and go over river and into Gloucestershire. At once
take path on right signed as 'Wye Valley Walk'. Go past the
woods of Lord's Grove to main road at Lower Redbrook
(once an industrial village and railway terminus). Cross to
B4231 – sharp climb now to Upper Redbrook. Bear left along
cart-track (signed as Offa's Dyke Path). Follow clear
waymarked path through meadows and climb to The Kymin.
Follow arrowed way to join lane for descent to Wye Bridge.
Retrace steps to carpark. Walk cannot be shortened.

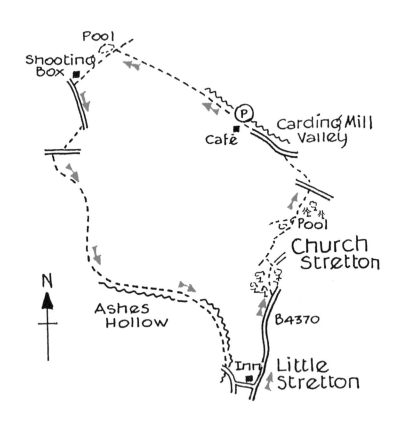

Pool

Shooting
Box

Carding Mill
Valley

Café

P

Pool

Church
Stretton

N

Ashes
Hollow

B4370

Inn

Little
Stretton

WALK 79

SHROPSHIRE

79. *Long Mynd (1)*

Distance of walk: 12km/7ml.
Distance from Birmingham: 73km/45ml.
Ordnance Survey maps: 137 and 910.
Refreshments: Café by start; inns and tea-rooms, Church
    Stretton; inn, Little Stretton.
Paths: Well-walked; few are waymarked; take care not to
    confuse with sheep tracks.
Terrain: Long Mynd covered with rocks and heather; tracks
    rough – steep in places.
Points of interest: National Trust owns 5,500 acres of open
    moorland; heather home for red grouse (most southerly
    grouse moor in England), ravens, dippers, buzzards; pre-
    historic sites, burial mounds and hill-forts on uplands;
    Bodbury Camp near highest point of golf course (one of
    the highest in England at 1,200ft); ancient highway (the
    Port Way) along top of Long Mynd.

This ridge of some of the oldest rocks in the land (pre-
Cambrian) rises from the plain to 1,700ft.
    Park at carpark in Carding Mill Valley near Church
Stretton. 443944. From carpark follow path which borders
brook upstream. Track crosses and recrosses water. Keep
climbing up valley to top of plateau. Turn left by pool
following a wide track. On lane (shooting box right) turn left.
Within third of a mile take track right to meet the Port Way.

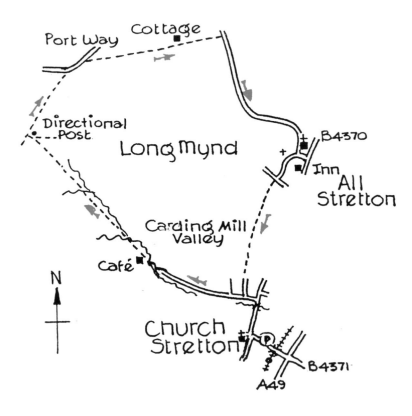

Port Way Cottage

Directional Post

Long Mynd

B4370

Inn

All Stretton

Carding Mill Valley

Café

N

Church Stretton

P

B4371

A49

WALK 80

Continue right. At Pole Cottage take track left. Drop downhill. Other paths are joined. Keep descending along Ashes Hollow – a valley. Near cottage leave NT lands. Walk through pastures and campsite to lane. Turn left then left again to B4370. Proceed left for half a mile. Take rough track left through woods to cul-de-sac lane. At once leave lane path on left. Climb steeply to stile. Turn right – track along rocky way. Descend to pool. Swing right – path by right-hand wood to road. Cross to opposite track to carpark.

To shorten walk: After turning left on lane by shooting box stay on lane to descend from Long Mynd. Save three miles.

80. *Long Mynd (2)*

Distance of walk: 12km/7ml.
Distance from Birmingham: 73km/45ml.
Ordance Survey maps: 137 and 910.
Refreshments: Cafés and inns, Church Stretton; café, Carding Mill Valley; inn, All Stretton.
Paths: Good, well-used tracks.
Terrain: Rocky with vast expanses of heather and tumbling brooks.
Points of interest: National Trust uplands; ancient highway – Port Way; Church Stretton church – Norman with twelfth-century tower.

The hump of the Long Mynd rises to 1,700ft and offers splendid walking. There are numerous ancient camps and tumuli. The area was described by Mary Webb in her novels; Church Stretton was Shepwardine.

Park in signed town carparks. 453941. Walk northwards along B4370. Take road left signed to Carding Mill Valley. Go past carparking areas and café. Keep ahead along rocky track which follows brook. At confluence of brooks take right-hand fork. Keep ahead when brook disappears, staying on clear track to wider way. Turn left to directional post. A few steps further turn right down vehicle-track. This is the Port Way. Follow way to lane by signpost. Follow direction signed Woolstaston. After cattle-grid (third of a mile) leave

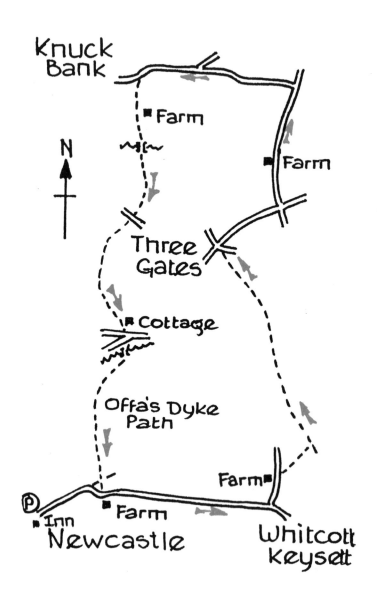

WALK 81

lane by taking signed bridleway right. Go past cottage to lane. Turn right to village of All Stretton. Just before main road turn right. Climb hill to a junction. Take opposite path over a footbridge to a meadow. At far end walk through kissing gate to house drive. Cross to pathway to common land. Take the clear upper track to a lane. Cross to opposite track. Way borders wood and becomes a lane to join outward route back to Church Stretton.

This walk cannot easily be shortened.

81. *Offa's Dyke (North)*

Distance of walk: 13km/8ml.
Distance from Birmingham: 96km/60ml.
Ordnance Survey maps: 137 and 930.
Refreshments: Inn, Newcastle.
Paths: Good, using Offa's Dyke Path and Shropshire Way.
Terrain: Undulating rough pasture, woods and lanes.
Points of interest: Archaeological feature of Offa's Dyke.

Offa (King of Mercia) built this ditch and bank to mark the border with Wales. It is now a long-distance path about 110 miles long and takes in some high hills along the way.

Park at roadside in Newcastle. 248823. From Newcastle walk along lane for two miles to Whitcott Keysett. Turn left at junction (signed Cefn Einion). Within quarter of a mile go through gate right. Climb to top of ridge. Turn left (now along waymarked Shropshire Way) to lane at Three Gates. Turn left then right at first crossroads and left at next. Continue to next junction. Turn left. Climb Knuck Bank (at 1,325ft). Here Offa's Dyke crosses lane. Turn left along waymarked path. Follow clear arrowed way (acorn signs) to lane by church. Turn right to Newcastle.

To shorten walk: Turn left at crossroads at Three Gates. Saves four miles.

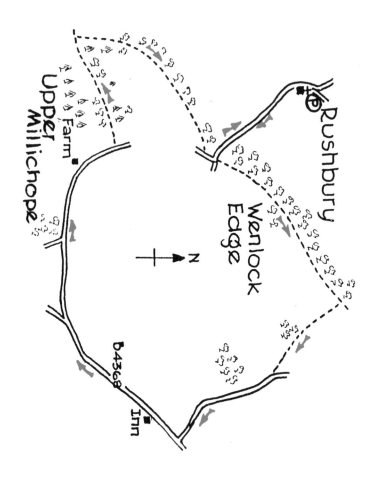

Rushbury

Upper Millichope

Farm

Wenlock Edge

N

b4368

Inn

WALK 82

82. *Wenlock Edge (1)*

Distance of walk: 13km/8ml.
Distance from Birmingham: 69km/43ml.
Ordnance Survey maps: 138 and 910.
Refreshments: Inn on route on B4368.
Paths: Good, well-used tracks.
Terrain: Uplands are mixture of woods, arable fields and sheep pastures.
Points of interest: Literary associations with Housman and Mary Webb (called these 'the hills of heaven'); Norman church and castle site, Rushbury.

Wenlock Edge is wooded ridge which was one of the hills immortalised by A.E. Housman in his narrative poem 'A Shropshire Lad'.

Park at roadside in Rushbury. 514919. From Rushbury take lane which climbs side of Wenlock Edge. At junction of lanes turn left along signed bridleway. Beyond houses keep ahead through hunting gate and along well-worn track. Walk through wood. Within one-and-a-half miles turn right over stile. Keep alongside border of field then wood. Keep at sides of further fields then along cart-track to lane. Turn right to B4368. Turn right. After one mile take lane on right. At junctions bear right (signed Rushbury) through Upper Millichope. Ignore bridleway by farm; half a mile further take another on left. Walk by plantations to farmstead. Through metal gate turn right through another gate. Follow track to Wenlock Edge. Through gates join farm vehicle-way. At junction of paths take waymarked route along right-hand fork. Pass cottages and continue to lane. Turn left.

To shorten walk: Keep ahead along lane at Upper Millichope saves one mile.

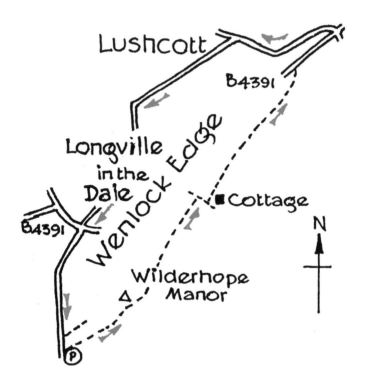

WALK 83

83. Wenlock Edge (2)

Distance of walk: 9km/6ml.
Distance from Birmingham: 69km/43ml.
Ordnance Survey maps: 138 and 910.
Refreshments: Inn, Longville.
Paths: Good, wide tracks.
Terrain: Limestone ridge which drains well and wooded
   scarp slopes.
Points of interest: Wilderhope Manor is rambling, gabled
   house dating from sixteenth century, now owned by
   National Trust and used as youth hostel; Wenlock Edge
   has inspired novelists, poets and musicians (e.g. Mary
   Webb and A.E. Housman).

Park on verge by track signed to Wilderhope. 539927. Walk
along track to Wilderhope Manor youth hostel. Keep along
vehicle track (once ancient road). Go past farm to T-junction
of tracks. Turn right. By cottage keep on main way which
turns 90 degrees left. The straight way (a right-of-way
bridleway) goes to Lutwyche Hall and B4371. Turn right to
road junction. Turn left. The lovely way drops sharply off the

Walk 85   The start of the walk at Bridges

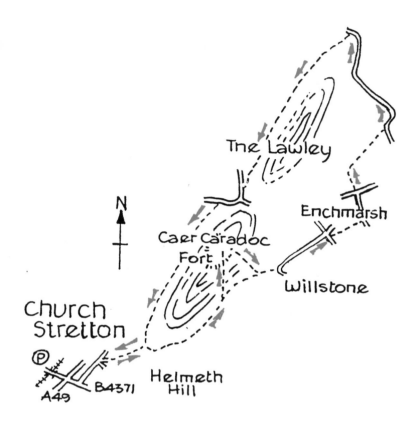

The Lawley

Enchmarsh

N

Caer Caradoc
Fort

Willstone

Church
Stretton

Ⓟ

A49

B4371

Helmeth
Hill

WALK 84

Edge through Easthope Wood to hamlet of Lushcott. Keep along lane to B4371 at Longville in the Dale. Cross almost directly over to cross dismantled railway and climb steep, wooded scarp edge. Just over brow is starting place.

This walk cannot be conveniently shortened.

84. Caer Caradoc

Distance of walk: 19km/12ml.
Distance from Birmingham: 75km/47ml.
Ordnance Survey maps: 137 and 910.
Refreshments: Inns and cafés, Church Stretton.
Paths: Rocky tracks not all marked.
Terrain: Mixed – rough moorland, woods and lanes.
Points of interest: Hill-fort occupied by Caractacus (AD 51);
   Norman church; Church Stretton nineteenth-century
   resort.

The walk climbs 1,500ft hill occupied by Caractacus before his last great battle against the Romans.

From carpark at Church Stretton (456937) cross A49 to B4371. Immediately turn left along road. After 500 yards take vehicle-way right (left of two). By entrance to New House Farm take rocky track right. Walk beneath Helmeth Hill to main track. Turn right then take one of the paths left to summit of Caer Caradoc. Descend to old main track and continue to lane at Willstone. Turn left then right at crossroads (signed Cardington). At once leave lane through metal gate and go along cart-track to lane. Turn left to T-junction at Enchmarsh. Go right then at once left along cart-track to lane. Turn left. After one-and-a-quarter miles take signed bridleway on left (signed 'Wellhouse'). At lane turn left then right at junction. After a few hundred yards take signed path on left. Path goes beneath Caer Caradoc.

To shorten walk: Turn left at Willstone crossroads (saves five miles).

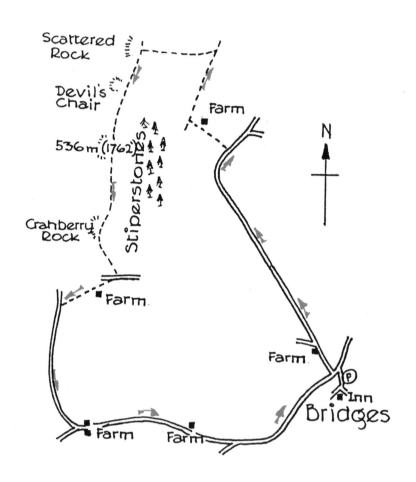

WALK 85

85. Stiperstones

Distance of walk: 11km/7ml.
Distance from Birmingham: 92km/58ml.
Ordnance Survey maps: 137 and 909.
Refreshments: Inn, Bridges.
Paths: Well-defined tracks.
Terrain: Route is over rocky uplands and pine woods; approach and return along narrow lanes.
Points of interest: Area features in books by Mary Webb; region rich in folklore – Stiperstones, Devil's Chair (weird-shaped rock), etc.

The walk is over rugged countryside with rocky tors of hard rock (of Ordovician period). The outcrops (highest 1,762ft) are often covered in mists. This was an area of lead mines and spoil heaps remain.

Park beside lane near inn at Bridges. 394964. Climb lane to road. Go over bridge then left then right along macadamed track. Climb to farm. Here way divides. Take right-hand fork. After beech-tree avenue, lane bends sharply right. Take lane left (signed to Hollies). At isolated farm keep ahead through gate. The rocky track goes to T-junction. Turn right. Through gate leave main track. Aim for stile left by holly bush over field left. Now on open moorland, climb heathered slopes to track which runs along top of Stiperstones ridge. Turn left to rocky outcrop of Devil's Chair, a tor surmounted by trig plinth and Cranberry Rock. (Note rocks said to have been hewn by convicts.) Keep on track which veers left to hunting gate. Continue to road. Walk few steps right. Bear left over heathland alongside fence. On lane turn left to pass farm to junction. Turn left to Bridges.

To shorten walk: Turn left on road after descending from Stiperstones ridge – saves two miles.

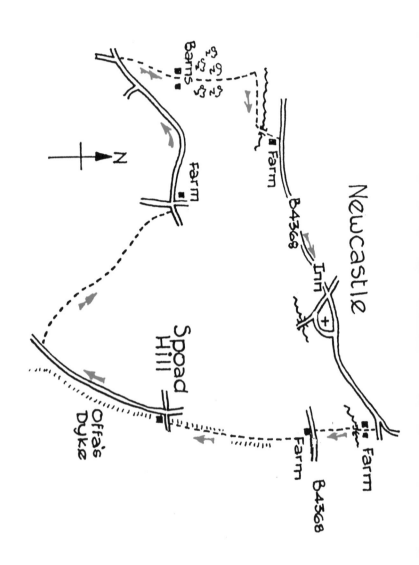

WALK 86

86.   *Spoad Hill*

Distance of walk: 12km/7ml.
Distance from Birmingham: 104km/65ml.
Ordnance Survey maps: 137 and 930/950.
Refreshments: Inn, Newcastle.
Paths: Good tracks; part of route is Offa's Dyke Path.
Terrain: Rocky, open countryside with mainly sheep-farming
    on uplands.
Points of interest: Well-preserved section of Offa's Dyke
    (built by King Offa around 1200 to mark border with
    Wales).

Spoad Hill is a plateau at about 1,300ft (400 metres) above
sea level. Offa's Dyke was strategically routed to make use
of the viewpoint.

Park in street at village of Newcastle. 248824. Leave
B4368 in centre of village and walk eastwards along lane. At
Y-junction keep right. A few steps further turn right through
meadow and farmyard, following Offa's Dyke Path
(waymarked with acorn emblem). Turn left to cross River
Clun. In field bear left to go over rivulet. Continue to lane and
farm at Lower Spoad. Follow marked way through farmyard.
Keep ahead to climb stile to left of farm track. Climb hillside
near good section of Dyke. A lane and farm are met on
summit of Spoad Hill. (Lane is part of ancient high ridgeway
track.) Turn right then left at crossroads. Cross straight over
(lane signed Bettws-y-Crwyn). Opposite second road on left
take farm track on right. Track descends to cross river and by
farm to B4368. Newcastle is to right.

To shorten walk: Turn right at last crossroads. Saves one-
and-a-half miles.

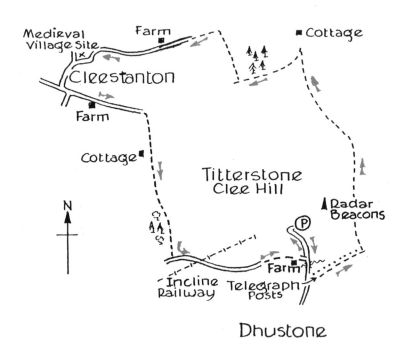

Medieval
Village Site

Farm

Cottage

Cleestanton

Farm

Cottage

Titterstone
Clee Hill

Radar
Beacons

N

P

Farm

Incline
Railway

Telegraph
Posts

Dhustone

WALK 87

87. Titterstone Clee Hill

Distance of walk: 10km/6.5ml.
Distance from Birmingham: 67km/38ml.
Ordnance Survey maps: 138 and 951.
Refreshments: Should be carried.
Paths: There are many animal tracks on the ground and
footpaths are not always defined. However, walk this route
in good weather and the summit of the hill with the radar
masts will always be in view.
Terrain: Bracken and heather hill with rocky sections.
Points of interest: Old quarry workings with traces of incline
railway; satellite tracking station on summit; medieval
village.

This hill is scarred with old quarries and what has been left
behind is not always attractive. The workings from many
centuries have all but obliterated the ancient hill-top fort but
not the view – the height is about 1,750ft.

Park at top of road from A4117 and Dhustone outside gates
marked 'Official Vehicles Only'. 594776. Admire view then
descend hill along road. Within third of a mile there is
junction of lanes. Path is just beyond on left – it is not clearly
defined but direction is marked by keeping telegraph poles on
left side. At fence turn left along track, aiming towards distant
cottage. Before cottage turn left. Follow alongside fence.
Walk at border of pine-wood (on right side). Keep ahead to
climb stile to field right. Walk to far gate to rough track.
Continue to junction of tracks. Turn left. Track becomes lane
and passes farms and site of medieval village (on right) to
hamlet of Cleestanton. Turn left at two T-junctions. Within
150 yards main road turns sharp right. Keep ahead along lane
signed as no-through road. Pass farm. Track turns right
through gate. Follow way to left of cottage and continue to
lane. Turn left to first junction of lanes. Climb hill to start.

The walk cannot be shortened.

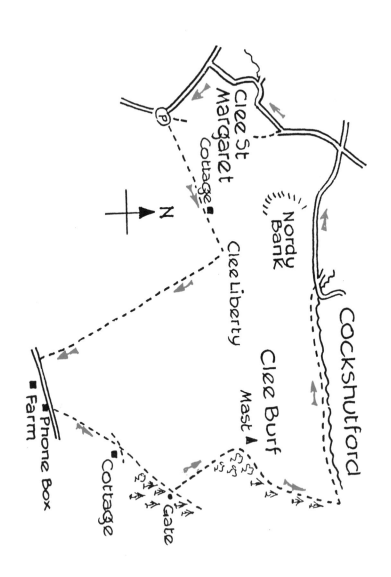

WALK 88

88.   Clee Burf

Distance of walk: 13km/8ml.
Distance from Birmingham: 74km/46ml.
Ordnance Survey maps: 138 and 931.
Refreshments: Should be carried.
Paths: Mostly well-used tracks but multiplicity of sheep runs on Clee Burf. Part of route along Shropshire Way (buzzard signs).
Terrain: Heather, turf and bracken on hills; dairy farms in valleys; evidence of old quarry workings.
Points of interest: Industrial archaeology (conveyor system for limestone – abandoned 1945); pretty village with ford at Clee St Margaret; ancient hill-forts on Clee Burf and Nordy Bank.

Clee Burf (one of the two summits of Brown Clee Hill) rises to 1,673ft and was a valuable source of limestone in the Second World War. There are no longer any active quarries on Brown Clee Hill.

Park at small carpark by Clee Liberty Common (along lane half a mile south-east from Clee St Margaret). 568838. Go over stile to common. Walk by right-hand border of common. Soon Nordy Bank hill-fort is seen away to left. Pass to right of cottage with fine weather vane. Still by border of common, continue along tractor route to climb step-stile by metal gate (Shropshire Way sign). Walk alongside fence and bushes (on right side). Keep on constant heading to descend along wide hedged way to lane. Turn left. Within third of a mile (opposite phone box) take signed path left. Climb steeply. Cross drive to isolated cottage to climb to two gates. Pass through left-hand one. Path is along sunken track but easier to walk along banktop. Keep ahead through next gate and alongside fence and wood (on right). At wooden gate leave fence. Turn 90 degrees left to strike out over heather. Aim for distant radio masts. Pass to right of masts. Go through gate. Walk alongside trees (on right) to gate in fence. Bear left. Drop down to valley. Turn left. Follow track bordering stream (on right) to Cockshutford. Turn left along

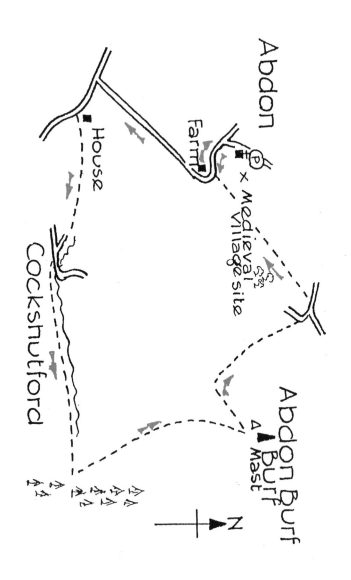

Abdon

Farm

Medieval village site

House

Cockshutford

Abdon Burf
Mast

N

WALK 89

lane (passing old limestone loading workings). At crossroads turn left to Clee St Margaret. Follow through village to T-junction. Turn left to carpark.

To shorten walk: Take bridleway along vehicle-way left after last crossroads. Saves one mile.

89. *Abdon Burf*

Distance of walk: 11km/7ml.
Distance from Birmingham: 74km/46ml.
Ordnance Survey maps: 139 and 931.
Refreshments: Should be carried.
Paths: Sheep runs on hills can conceal paths but route easily followed. Path to Cockshutford often boggy. Part of route along Shropshire Way.
Terrain: Heather and turf on hills with rocky outcrops; mixed pasture and arable lands on lower lands.
Points of interest: Hill-forts on summit of Abdon Burf and Nordy Bank; traces of medieval village near Abdon.

Abdon Burf is the highest hill in Shropshire at 1,772ft. There has been much mining and quarrying over the centuries – for limestone, iron, coal and basalt (for road building), etc. – but all has now ceased and the countryside reverted to nature.

There is limited parking by little church at Abdon village. 575867. Walk to T-junction. Turn left (signed Clee St Margaret). Continue along lane to crossroads. Turn left for quarter of a mile. Just past house turn left along rough vehicle-way. Track is soon squeezed along muddy way between fences and sheep pasture. On constant heading go through gates and over fence-stile. Continue to farmstead. Walk along drive to lane at Cockshutford. Turn left for few steps. Take vehicle-way right. Climb stile. Follow near left-hand brook to top of valley and trees. Here swing left having joined Shropshire Way (marked by buzzard emblems). Go through gate and veer right along path. Continue to masts at summit of hill. Drop downhill in south-west direction to fence. Pass through gap. Follow Shropshire Way signs to gate to sunken track. This goes through rough pastureland to

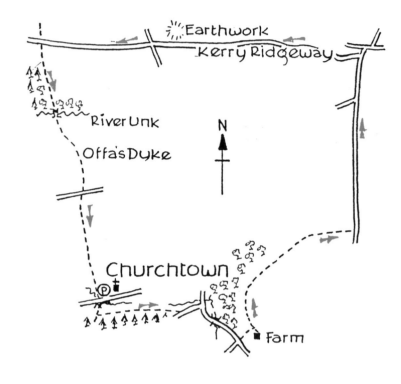

Earthwork

Kerry Ridgeway

River Unk

Offa's Dyke

N

Churchtown

Farm

WALK 90

fence-stile by gate to lane. Keep ahead to T-junction. Turn left (signed Abdon). Within 100 yards climb stile left. Take arrowed direction alongside left-hand wire fence. Series of stiles shows way to crossing of brook. Vehicle-way goes to lane at Abdon. Turn right and retrace steps to church.

This walk cannot be shortened.

90. Kerry Ridgeway

Distance of walk: 10km/6.5ml.
Distance from Birmingham: 96km/60ml.
Ordnance Survey maps: 137 and 930.
Refreshments: Should be carried.
Paths: Good, well-waymarked route.
Terrain: Fine, undulating countryside through pastural farmland and woods.
Points of interest: Good section of Offa's Dyke; isolated stone church at Churchtown; ancient earthworks along Kerry Ridgeway.

The walk is unique in using four long-distance routes – the Offa's Dyke Path, Shropshire Way, the Kerry Ridgeway and Wild Edric's Way. It is also in one of the ten Environmentally Sensitive Areas (ESAs) of England and Wales designated to protect the countryside from damage caused by changes in farming practice.

Park in the lane (take care not to block accesses) near old church at Churchtown. 263874. Cross nearby footbridge over brook along Offa's Dyke Path going south. Walk through pine plantation to step-stile to woods. At once turn left to climb another stile (marked with buzzard emblem – Shropshire Way waymark). Walk at edge of woods (bluebells in spring) to emerge on lane. Turn left to T-junction. Turn right. At next junction turn left through gate. Walk along banked way. Through gate turn left. Within yards way divides. Take right fork along tractor-way to top-right gate. Walk along wide hedged way. After three-quarters of a mile bear right. Walk along fenced way lined with bushes to gates to lane. Turn left. Keep ahead at first junction. At next

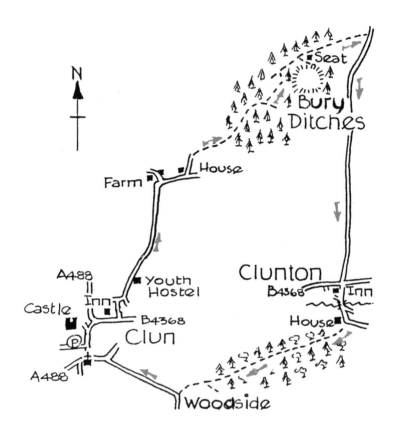

WALK 91

junction turn left (signed Hopton). This lane is Kerry Ridgeway. Keep ahead at crossroads. One mile further turn left over stile. Continue along Offa's Dyke Path. Follow clear route waymarked by acorn emblems. Cross lane. Churchtown is at next lane.

To shorten walk: Turn left at junction before Kerry Ridgeway junction. Saves one mile.

91. Bury Ditches

Distance of walk: 16km/10ml.
Distance from Birmingham: 96km/60ml.
Ordnance Survey maps: 137 and 930.
Refreshments: Inns, Clun and Clunton.
Paths: Good tracks. Part of route along Shropshire Way and
    Jack Mytton Way (waymarked bridleway).
Terrain: Route on hills both sides of River Clun is along lanes
    through pastoral lands and Forestry Commission conifer
    woods.
Points of interest: Bury Ditches (ancient hill-fort) cover
    extensive earthworks on top of wooded hill; ruin of Clun's
    Norman castle; youth hostel in former mill; ancient five-
    arched bridge at Clun.

From carpark near bridge on south side of river (299807) cross river. Turn right along main street (B4368). Turn left (Ford Street) following YHA signs. Turn right at T-junction. Follow lane past youth hostel. Lane passes extensive farmstead after one-and-a-quarter miles. Lane becomes rough track and swings sharp left by house. Follow vehicle-track to pass through gate (Shropshire Way buzzard waymark) to Forestry Commission woods. Keep along main forest 'road' ignoring other tracks and 'roads'. After half a mile 'road' twists sharp right. Take grassy track left climbing past waymark post with red ring. At summit turn left to T-junction of tracks. Turn right and continue climbing. At next junction keep ahead (but turn right for route marked by red ring posts to Bury Ditches) to pass to left of seat. Wide track descends to stile to pasture. Maintain direction through fields

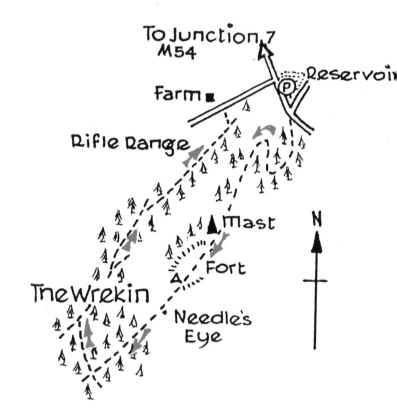

To Junction 7
M54

Reservoir

Farm ■

Rifle Range

Mast

Fort

The Wrekin

Needle's Eye

N

WALK 92

to gate to lane. Turn right to Clunton. Cross to opposite lane. Within quarter of a mile lane twists sharp left. Take path right just beyond white cottage through wicket gate. Follow bridleway at edge of woods (Jack Mytton Way) to join rough tractor-way. Follow this to lane. Turn right. Follow lanes to Clun.

This walk cannot be shortened.

92. *The Wrekin*

Distance of walk: 7km/4.5ml.
Distance from Birmingham: 56km/35ml.
Ordnance Survey maps: 127 and 890.
Refreshments: Should be carried.
Paths: Well-used tracks; part of route along Shropshire Way.
Terrain: Rocky outcrops although most of hill is clothed in
　　conifer woods.
Points of interest: Ancient hill-fort on summit; distinctive
　　rocks with such names as Needle's Eye; reservoir
　　(gathering place for wildfowl); Wrekin is famous 'beacon'
　　hill (Macaulay wrote 'Streamed in crimson on the wind
　　the Wrekin's crest of light').

Park in parking place bordering lane at junction of lanes near reservoir one mile south of Junction 7 of M54. 093637. Take signed footpath over stile by gate at junction of lanes. Walk along broad track, gradually climbing through woods. Keep ahead at junctions of tracks. Pass gates and stile, continuing to climb to summit (TV mast and trig. plinth at 1,334ft) along stony track. Keep on same heading along footpath, passing Needle's Eye and rocks. After sharp descent turn right at wide crossing track. Many other tracks but keep direction. At T-junction turn right. Take left fork then right fork at Y-junctions. Pass rifle range – observe warning notices. Beyond range (near warning notice) bold track is met. Keep ahead for few steps. Turn left (Shropshire Way buzzard emblem) through hedge gap. Cross field to step-stile to lane. Turn right to carpark.

This walk cannot be shortened.

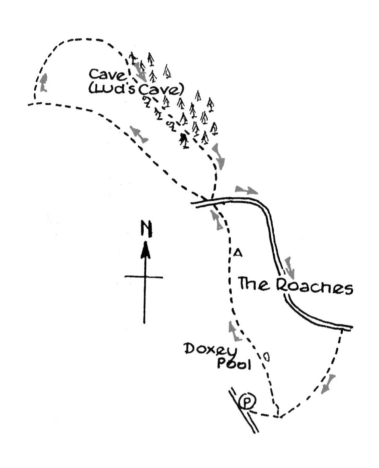

Cave!
(Lud's Cave)

N

The Roaches

Doxey
Pool

WALK 93

STAFFORDSHIRE

93. The Roaches

Distance of walk: 11km/7ml.
Distance from Birmingham: 96km/60ml.
Ordnance Survey maps: 118/119 and 792 and Outdoor
    Leisure no. 24 (The Peak District).
Refreshments: Should be carried.
Paths: Good ways but beware sheep tracks. Part of route is
    along Staffs. Moorlands Walk.
Terrain: Paths over hard rock – drains well.
Points of interest: Watching rock climbers; rocky hollow of
    Lud's church (witchcraft associations).

The western boundary of the Peak District includes the
craggy ridge known as The Roaches (perhaps from French
les rochers – the rocks). The cliffs rise to 1,600ft and have
been a training ground for noted mountaineers.

Use roadside carpark at The Roaches. 004621. From
carpark take way through nearby gate. Near bottom of cliffs
turn left. Past cottage turn right to walk through scattered
rocks. Climb steeply and bear right up steps. Bear left. Walk
through scattered boulders. At path sign continue right to
reach summit of The Roaches. Turn left along ridge. Keep to
left of pool. Pass trig plinth. Keep on main path to lane at
Roach End. Cross to opposite path. Walk alongside wall.
Keep on path to walk along ridge path. Drop down to
meeting of paths. Take way signed Gradbach to right. When

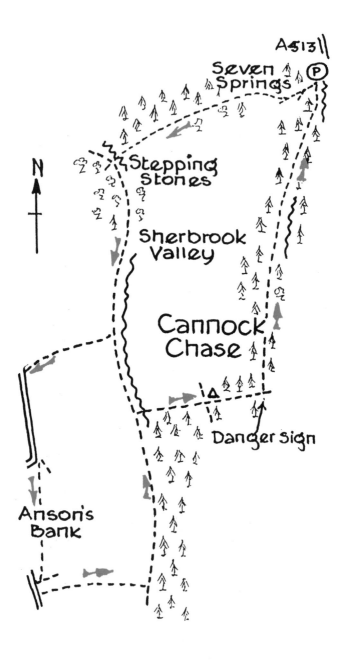

A513

Seven
Springs

P

Stepping
Stones

Sherbrook
Valley

Cannock
Chase

Danger Sign

N

Anson's
Bank

WALK 94

path divides take way signed 'Lud's Church'. Walk along hollow. Climb steps. Swing left to good path through wood. Follow way signed Roach End. Out of trees keep ahead. Over stone stile join cart-track to Roach End. Take Staffs. Moorlands Walk. Pass houses and after one-and-a-half miles take farm track over cattle-grid right. Track climbs then divides – take right way. Climb stile adjoining gate. Aim for far gate. Do not pass through but climb stile right. Follow path to outward track to carpark.

To shorten walk: Omit second circle of the figure-of-eight route – saves two-and-a-half miles.

94.   Cannock Chase (North)

Distance of walk: 13km/8ml.
Distance from Birmingham: 48km/30ml.
Ordnance Survey maps: 127, 128 and 891, 892.
Refreshments: Nearest inn at Milford (one-and-a-half miles off route).
Paths: Good, clear tracks – many forest 'roads'; part of route along Staffs. Way.
Terrain: Cannock Chase is of acid and sandy soils; tracks are boggy in places; route crosses open heathland and pine forests.
Points of interest: Fallow deer; wildlife; alder trees in Sherbrook Valley once used for clog making; clear, shallow streams; picnic sites.

Cannock Chase was, from Norman times, a favourite royal hunting ground. Today there are many herds of fallow deer of a species brought to England by the Romans. Much of the old forest was felled during the Industrial Revolution for use as charcoal but pockets of ancient oaks remain. There are many acres of Forestry Commission plantations.

Park at carpark off A513 at Seven Springs. 002207. Pass through barrier in top-right corner of carpark. Keep on right-hand track and go through another barrier. Again take right-hand track. Path is between pine plantations to junction of paths by brook at 'Stepping Stones'. Turn left along wide

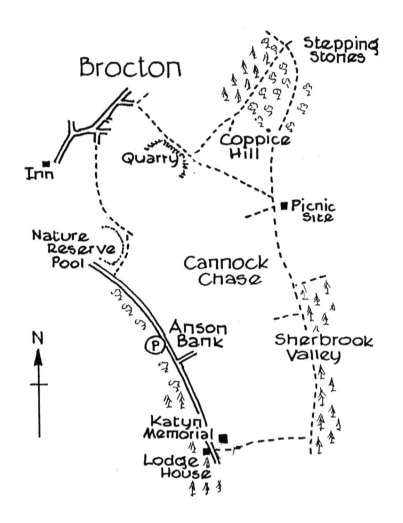

Brocton

Stepping Stones

Quarry

Coppice Hill

Inn

Picnic Site

Nature Reserve Pool

Cannock Chase

Anson Bank

N

Sherbrook Valley

Katyn Memorial

Lodge House

WALK 95

track signed Staffs. Way. Walk along valley with stream to left. At pools and picnic benches bear right (still Staffs. Way signs) to road. Turn left. Within half a mile (on bend) keep ahead along track over Anson's Bank (named after the admiral). Keep ahead at road then at once turn left (signed Katyn Memorial) along track to wide way by pine plantation. Turn left. After mile go right to keep pines on right side. Climb to junction of tracks. Keep ahead also at next crossing on forest 'road'. Drop down to 'danger' post and turn left to Seven Springs.

To shorten walk: Keep ahead by pools and picnic benches. Saves three miles.

95. Cannock Chase (East)

Distance of walk: 11km/7ml.
Distance from Birmingham: 48km/30ml.
Ordnance Survey maps: 127 and 871.
Refreshments: Nearest inn half a mile off route at Brockton.
Paths: Good, well-walked tracks.
Terrain: Sandy heathlands and pine plantations. Some road walking.
Points of interest: Katyn Memorial; Brocton Nature Reserve; old oak forest remnant; picnic sites.

Cannock Chase was once a sheep-rearing centre with a distinctive type of grey-faced sheep which roamed the high uplands among the old oak trees. The great forests are now heathlands with many plantations of Scots and Corsican pines.

Park at carpark at Anson's Bank. 975176. Walk south-east along road for one mile. Opposite lodge house turn left along track signed to Katyn Memorial. Keep ahead past carpark and continue to Sherbrook Valley. Turn left with large pine plantations on right side. Continue ahead and through birch-woods for two-and-a-half miles, passing picnic site. At junction of wide tracks called Stepping Stones take path on left (signed Coppice Hill). There is steep climb with other paths joining. Stay on main track. At top of hill bear right at

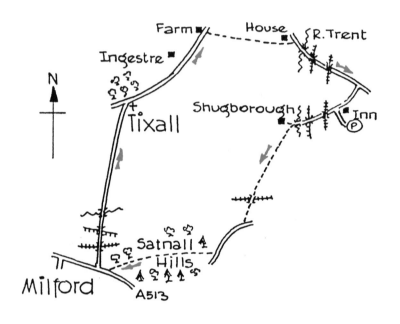

WALK 96

Y-junction. Maintain heading through carpark to directional post. Take unsigned way right alongside cliff (on left). Keep ahead on main track to road. Turn left to Brockton. Go by green and along Old Acre Lane. At end pass through kissing gate. Keep on main track through beech trees to pool of nature reserve. Turn left (water on right) follow bankside to another path. Turn right over plank bridge. Immediately leave main track to turn right alongside fence above pool. Drop down bank to road. Turn left to carpark.

To shorten walk: Just after picnic site in Sherbrook Valley take path on left. Saves two miles.

96. *Satnall Hills*

Distance of walk: 9km/6ml.
Distance from Birmingham: 48km/30ml.
Ordnance Survey maps: 127 and 871.
Refreshments: Inns, Great Haywood; inns and cafés, Milford.
Paths: Good tracks through woods and over farmland; part of route uses Staffordshire Way long-distance path.
Terrain: Parkland of Shugborough; sandy soils in woodland.
Points of interest: Shugborough Hall – home of Anson family since 1624, now National Trust and housing museum; fourteenth-century packhorse bridge; garden follies in park; Staffs. and Worcester Canal; Tudor gatehouse of Ingrestre.

The Satnall Hills are part of Cannock Chase and are clothed in attractive woodlands.

Limited streetside parking in village of Great Haywood. 998229. By the Clifford Arms Inn go down cul-de-sac street. Go under railway and over canal. Walk along packhorse bridge (longest in England). Enter grounds of Shugborough Hall (house on right). Keep ahead along estate road to cross railway. On main road turn right for third of a mile. Take path on right signed as over Satnall Hills. Follow track through woods. On main road again turn right to Milford Common. Turn right along lane signed to Tixall. Cross railway and

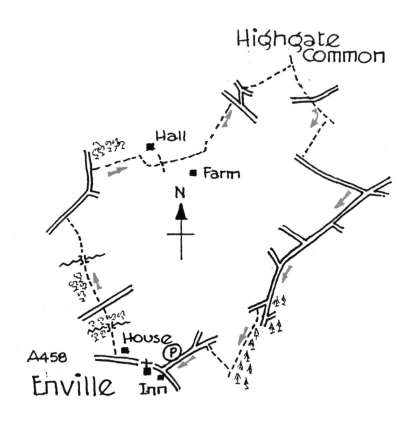

WALK 97

River Sow. Keep ahead through Tixall (old gatehouse on left). Opposite farm and by gatehouse take signed bridleway on right. Keep ahead to gate on to road by cottage (mill nearby). Turn right to Great Haywood.

This walk cannot be shortened.

97. *Highgate Common*

Distance of walk: 13km/8ml.
Distance from Birmingham: 29km/18ml.
Ordnance Survey maps: 138/139 and 933.
Refreshments: Inn, Enville.
Paths: Good but multiplicity of tracks on common; part of route along Staffs. Way.
Terrain: Sandy soils on common but clay on lower ground can be muddy in winter.
Points of interest: Enville Hall (nineteenth-century Gothic house); unusual turreted tower of Enville church; Elizabethan Mere Farm.

The walk climbs through farmland to the plateau common. The wide expanse of heathland is fun for youngsters who love to fly kites on the breezy heights.

Streetside parking off main road. 825868. From Enville village walk along A458 past church. Within 400 yards turn right down footpath – path signed at side of house drive. Walk at edge of grass to white metal gate in far corner. Keep ahead through trees and wood then at border of field to lane. Cross to opposite path (signed as Staffs. Way). Maintain same general direction over stream and continue to road. Turn right and keep ahead at junction. Two hundred yards further turn right – footpath signed (Highgate Common) over stile. Walk on waymarked route past Mere Hall (farm to right). Follow cart-track to lane. Turn right then left (Gospel Oak Lane).

By road junction turn right along signed bridleway to Highgate Common. Turn right along track signed as red waymarked route. Keep ahead (ignoring other tracks) to reach carpark then lane. Cross directly over (now on brown

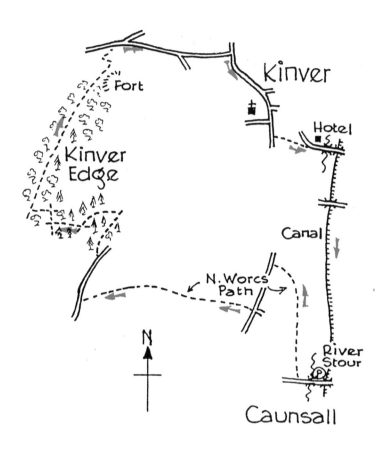

Kinver

Fort

Kinver
Edge

Hotel

Canal

N. Worcs
Path

N

River
Stour

Caunsall

WALK 98

waymarked route). Within 400 yards leave 'brown route' to continue half-right. Bridleway cuts across other tracks to lane. Turn left to climb hill. At junction turn right. Keep on road for one-and-a-half miles, passing junctions. When road divides bear right (Blundies Lane). Within 400 yards take cart-track on left. Keep at edge of pine-woods. After half a mile take farm track right. This goes to Enville.

This walk cannot be easily shortened.

98.   Kinver Edge

Distance of walk: 13km/8ml.
Distance from Birmingham: 35km/22ml.
Ordnance Survey maps: 138/139 and 933.
Refreshments: Inns and cafés, Kinver.
Paths: Good, waymarked tracks; part of route along North Worcs. Path, Staffs. Way and towpath of Staffs. and Worcs. Canal.
Terrain: The pine-and-birch-clothed Kinver uplands are of sandstone which drains well; lower part of route can be muddy at times.
Points of interest: Extensive earthworks of hill-fort; cave dwellings; National Trust lands; fourteenth-century Kinver church.

Kinver Edge is a fine wooded escarpment which gives lovely views along its length. It is criss-crossed with paths and here several long-distance paths meet. The rock houses were occupied until the 1950s.

Park near canal at hamlet of Caunsall. 853809. Alternatively, start the walk at Kinver Edge (carpark). Walk away from the canal and cross the River Stour. Within a few yards path (signed as North Worcs. Path) starts over stile by house drive right. Follow clear path to road. Turn left. Within third of a mile take bridleway along fenced way right. Keep ahead to lane. Turn right to lands of country park. Go into woods and through barrier. Follow yellow-arrowed way to carpark. Turn left through barrier; follow waymarked route signed as Worcs. Way and North Worcs. Path.

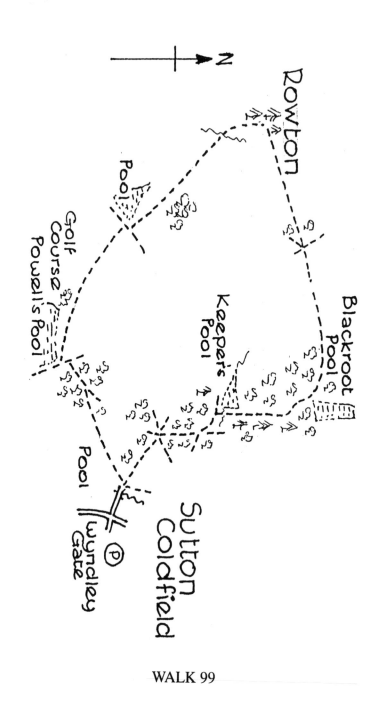

WALK 99

Track is through pines to crossroads of routes. Take signed way right. At next meeting of tracks (coppiced trees here) turn right. Path borders new plantations of trees. Pass through barrier. Turn left to top of ridge of Kinver Edge. Turn right (Staffs. Way). Pass trig plinth (600ft). Keep on Staffs. Way to descend scarp edge near rock houses along twisting path to road. Turn right to Kinver village. Walk along main street. As road twists left keep ahead along lane signed to Caunsall. Go past junction and take path signed up bank left. Follow pathway to descend pasture to kissing gate to lane. Turn right to hotel. Keep ahead along vehicle-track to canal. Turn right along towpath to road bridge at Caunsall.

This walk cannot be conveniently shortened.

99. *Rowton Hill (Sutton Park)*

Distance of walk: 6.5km/4ml.
Distance from Birmingham: 13km/8ml.
Ordnance Survey maps: 139 and 913.
Refreshments: Inns and cafés, Sutton Coldfield; kiosks in Sutton Park.
Paths: Good, well-marked tracks.
Terrain: Walk over sandy heathland – heather, gorse and woods (pine and deciduous).
Points of interest: Near route of Roman road (Icknield Street); interesting pools (Blackroot Pool – powered mills; Keeper's Pool built by John Holte in reign of Henry VI to stock fish).

Sutton Park is 2,400 acres of splendid wild grandeur which was a gift to Bishop Vesey from King Henry VIII in 1528. The Bishop gave it to the townsfolk. The walk climbs to about 530ft to give fine views.

Park either in Sutton Coldfield town carparks or in parking areas in Sutton Park. Enter the park at Wyndley Gate. 115957. Walk over bridge across brook. Turn left along park 'road' towards Powell's Pool. At T-junction continue left to pool. Turn right off 'road'. Gradually leave edge of water. Keep to right of golf course through scrubland to land. Cross

215

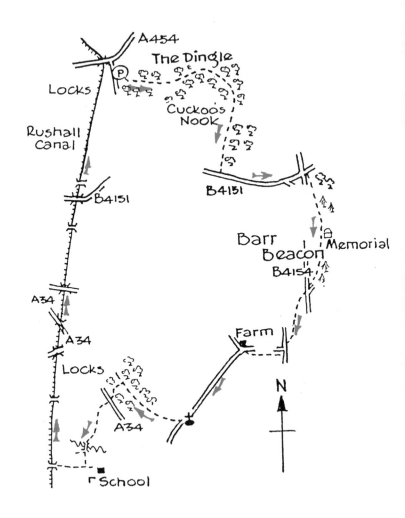

WALK 100

directly over. Make for point to left of circular fir/birch wood then aim towards clump of Scots pines on Rowton Hill. Turn right along broad track. Keep ahead at junction of ways and at crossing tracks. Walk through woods to Blackroot Pool. Swing right to Keeper's Pool. Go over causeway. Turn left. Walk through holly bushes of Holly Hurst and continue along tracks and park roads to Wyndley Gate.

This walk cannot conveniently be shortened.

100. Barr Beacon.

Distance of walk: 13km/8ml.
Distance from Birmingham: 13km/8ml.
Ordnance Survey maps: 139 and 913.
Refreshments: Should be carried.
Paths: Barr Beacon Way and canal towpath used.
Terrain: Barr Beacon is on sandstone heathland ridge. Route
  through woods, along lanes and by canal.
Points of interest: war memorial – built 1930s – (sadly
  vandalised) on Barr Beacon; Great Barr church dates from
  1677; Rushall Canal a late waterway of Canal Age (early
  nineteenth century) used to convey coal; Hayhead Wood
  Nature Reserve; the Dingle (once limestone quarry) pretty
  with bluebells in springtime; Cuckoo's Nook is fine wood
  where foxes roam.

Barr Beacon is one of highest points in the West Midlands at 744ft. Beacon fires used to be lit at the top to send news across the country. Now forms regional country park.

Walk starts at Hayhead Wood Nature Reserve carpark a short distance along Longwood Lane from canal bridge on A454. 041990. Follow sign into wood – Barr Beacon Way. At pool (canal branch for lime works) turn left. Follow well-waymarked way (also nature trail) beside brook. Route through the Dingle and Cuckoo's Nook then by Birch Wood to B4151. Turn left. Path runs beside road. Cross at traffic lights. Few steps further path is signed right to Barr Beacon. Beyond carpark follow path to road. Cross to opposite path to road by junction. Cross to Chapel Lane opposite. Path beside lane then along lane. Just past church take path through gateway right. Walk along avenue (once carriage ride of Barr Hall) into woods. Look for path signed left through trees to road. Cross to opposite path (still Beacon Way) to cross railing bridge. Bear left to school playing field. Turn right to canal. Take towpath northwards. At A454 cross canal. Take lane right to carpark.

This walk cannot easily be shortened.

Walk 91   The old mill youth hostel at Clun

AUTHOR'S COMMENTS
AND HINTS

The start

It is assumed that travel to the start is by car. Sadly, public transport in rural areas is now so denuded and infrequent that it cannot be relied on to reach the areas covered by the walking routes.

The distance to the starts from Birmingham is merely an approximate indication as of course there will be variation in the approach roads used.

The carparking for each walk is marked on the sketch maps. If the parking is on the road do please ensure that no accesses are blocked. And don't forget to take good care of your car keys on the ramble!

Walking alone or with companions?

This, naturally, is purely a matter of personal choice. Many love the peace and solitude of walking alone. However, one should always remember that even on the lowest and gentlest of hills accidents such as falls and sprains can occur. It is prudent therefore to let others be aware of your route and approximate time of return.

Personally, I think that the pleasures of walking country ways are best shared. Rambling clubs are thriving – some even have a membership waiting list because numbers are so great. If folk are lonely or depressed I do advise them to join a club. The friendship is infectious and even the most withdrawn or shy cannot avoid conversation on the walk, even to comment upon the weather – usually (but not always) sunny, of course. I am lucky to have a wife who also enjoys rambling. On the trek we always talk – time for communication is often missing in today's busy family routines.

Clothing and equipment

Like all sports and pastimes, the range of purpose-made clothing and equipment available for hill walking is vast. However, it should be stressed that no one needs to rush down to the outdoor-pursuit shops and spend a vast amount of money.

The essentials are firstly sound and comfortable footwear (boots or walking shoes). Boots have recently undergone a revolution. No longer need they be of gargantuan weight. Nowadays they can be surprisingly light (with attractive colouring for the fashion conscious!).

Next, waterproof clothing – even in the summer be prepared for bad weather and carry a good cagoule or anorak and waterproof over-trousers. So a rucksack is also needed, although this need not be vast for a day's outing.

Always remember that even though the weather may be warm and kind in the valley, the hills and moors can be cool and bleak so take a spare thick jumper. Other items of clothing to consider are waterproof gaiters, for keeping the ankles and feet dry (but I give these a miss), and gloves and scarves.

Safety equipment to pop in the preferably lightweight rucksack (framed or otherwise) includes the following: a compass (become familiar with its use at home), a small first-aid kit, a torch (with spare batteries), a whistle to use in emergencies (six short blows is the signal) and energy-giving foods such as chocolate or glucose tablets.

Maps

Always try to take a suitable map of the area you are covering – the Ordnance Survey 1:50,000 Landranger Series is recommended. For wet weather carry it in a transparent map case slung around your neck, although a simple office transparent folder is a good substitute.

The reference to the 1:25,000 Pathfinder Series Ordnance Survey map is given for each walk. These give the precise line of the paths but to have a complete set to cover all the walks described is an unessential, high-cost luxury.

Food and drink

There is a convenient pub on most of the routes. However, you are certain to work up an appetite and thirst on a ramble and many prefer in any case to wine and dine out of doors. A thermos flask of hot soup or coffee is always welcome. Remember that cans of drink are very heavy.

Weather

The rules are be prepared and use common sense. Listen to the local forecasts but do not be deterred if they sound unpromising – winter walking can be exhilarating if you are properly dressed and equipped. Always take care and adhere to sensible safety rules, especially in mists on the hills when frequent compass checks should be made. Ensure sufficient time is allowed for the walk, especially in winter. Keep a dry set of clothes in the car if the forecast is for inclement weather.

Rights and responsibilities

I have ensured to the best of my ability that all the routes are along public rights of way. However, please remember that rights of way can be legally diverted (or sometimes deleted from the Definitive Map) so do be prepared for changes. The countryside, too, is constantly changing which may affect the route description. Meadows may be ploughed, hedges removed, stiles erected or taken down, woods felled and so on.

Although walkers have the legal right of passage along a

right of way, remember that you are enjoying the privilege of walking over someone's private land. This privilege should not therefore be abused. There is a country saying that on a visit 'take nothing but photographs and leave nothing but footprints'. The lovely flora and fauna should be left untouched for others to enjoy and no litter left behind.

Great care should be taken with paths over farmland. If a path is across growing crops or ploughed land, the farmer should legally have reinstated the line of the path. Unfortunately this law is often flouted but always walk across the field in single file. Walls should not be climbed; always close gates and keep dogs under control.

INDEX